Talking about Cultural Diversity in Your Church

Gifts and Challenges

Michael V. Angrosino

ALTAMIRA
PRESS

A Division of
ROWMAN & LITTLEFIELD PUBLISHERS, INC.
Walnut Creek • Lanham • New York • Oxford

ALTAMIRA PRESS
A Division of Rowman & Littlefield Publishers, Inc.
1630 North Main Street, #367
Walnut Creek, CA 94596
www.altamirapress.com

Rowman & Littlefield Publishers, Inc.
4720 Boston Way
Lanham, MD 20706

12 Hid's Copse Road
Cumnor Hill, Oxford OX2 9JJ, England

British Library Cataloguing-in-Publication Information Available

Library of Congress Cataloging-in-Publication Data

Angrosino, Michael V.
    Talking about cultural diversity in your church : gifts and challenges / Michael
Angrosino.
        p.   cm.
    Includes bibliographical references and index.
    ISBN 0-7591-0180-9 (alk. paper)—ISBN 0-7591-0179-5 (pbk. : alk. paper)
    1. Christianity and culture. 2. Multiculturalism—Religious aspects—Christianity—Case
studies. I. Title.

BR115.C8 A46 2001
261.5—dc21

2001022770

Printed in the United States of America

♾™ The paper used in this publication meets the minimum requirements of American
National Standard for Information Sciences—Permanence of Paper for Printed Library
Materials, ANSI/NISO Z39.48-1992.

Contents

101607

Acknowledgments

Although I accept the responsibility for the final text of this workbook, I gratefully acknowledge the assistance, input, guidance, and support of the many people without whom the book could not have come to fruition. Special thanks go to all those who have participated in the workshops from which the material in this book derives, and who took the time to offer valuable insights that have made the process both more productive and more enjoyable for all concerned. I also thank Mitch Allen and Erik Hanson of AltaMira Press, who provided strong encouragement and constructive criticism as the book itself took form. I am grateful, too, to the several anonymous reviewers whose comments contributed greatly to the strengthening of both the organization and the contents of the book. Martha Ryltoff and Dennis Garber provided particular assistance with the development of the ideas in the chapter on intercultural communication.

I am most particularly grateful to Ruth Eileen Dwyer, S.P., Claudette Dwyer, Alexa Suelzer, S.P., and the rest of the faculty of the Master of Arts in Pastoral Theology program at Saint Mary-of-the-Woods College, to my fellow students in the MAPT program, and to the members of the Ministers of Providence, without whose guidance and support neither the workshops nor this workbook would ever have come to pass.

Introduction
THE CHALLENGE OF CULTURAL DIVERSITY

We live in a world in which traditional local boundaries have been blurred almost beyond recognition by the forces of modern transportation and communications media. Our own country, always a destination for people from far and wide, is no longer a place of relatively isolated, homogeneous enclaves (if it ever truly was). There is virtually nowhere we can go without having to deal with people who are different from us to a greater or lesser degree. We refer to this situation as one of cultural diversity, in the sense that we are exposed most of the time and in most situations to people who in onez way or another think, dress, talk, and act in ways that diverge from what we think is the norm—which we tend to define as however *we* think, dress, talk, and act.

One possible response to cultural diversity is to retreat behind the defensive borders of what we presume to be "our kind of people." But unless one lives with one's immediate family on a self-sufficient plot of land deep in the wilderness, it is highly unlikely that such a strategy can ever really work. And the frustration of struggling to make it work in more complex circumstances more often than not leads to the sort of ugly confrontations that we know as "ethnic cleansing" and civil war in other countries, and as "racial unrest" in cities in our own country. It therefore makes more sense to think of ways in which the apparent barriers to communication and cooperation represented by cultural diversity can be overcome—a goal far easier to state than to accomplish.

The difficulty in dealing with cultural diversity derives, at least in part, from simple misinformation, misunderstanding, and stereotyped evaluations of others. Cultural diversity itself is not a "problem," although problems often arise in situations of cultural diversity because of the following:

1. *Lack of knowledge* (resulting in an inability to recognize differences)
2. *Self-protection or denial* (leading to an attitude that differences are not significant, or that our common humanity transcends our differences)
3. *Fear of the unknown or the new* (because it is challenging and perhaps intimidating to get to understand something that is new, that does not fit into one's worldview)
4. *Feelings of pressure due to time or other constraints* (which can lead to feeling rushed to make important decisions and frustration at the complexities of looking at the issues in depth)

We must also keep in mind that, our best intentions aside, culturally diverse societies are prone to various forms of political and economic competition that make cooperation seem an unrealistic goal.

People sometimes think that the best way to deal with uncomfortable situations is to ignore them. But cultural diversity in the modern world is not going to disappear and we are not going to be able to understand diversity and develop competence in dealing with it simply by waiting for us all spontaneously to get along. It is important to develop the skills that will allow us to speak up and address perceived problems in a context of cultural diversity, and to do so responsibly and not in a spirit of mindless venting, complaining, or blaming. One diversity training workshop sponsored by my university is addressed to the "courageous messenger" who learns these skills and applies them successfully in the workplace. The failure, deliberate or otherwise, to become "courageous messengers" has such disruptive consequences that it would seem to be in our best interest to do what we can to find a better resolution than wishful thinking. And, indeed, cultural diversity is by no means beyond our capacities to understand and to incorporate successfully into our everyday lives. Studying cultural diversity has become an important focus for cultural anthropologists, sociologists, and other social scientists. Professionals involved in business, education, health and human services, athletics, and many other fields of endeavor have been busy applying the insights of those social scientists so as to train their members first in cultural sensitivity and then in the acquisition of true intercultural competence.

This book, however, is addressed specifically to professionals in the field of religion. Discussions of cultural diversity are far from unknown among religious professionals, but the issue is perhaps even more vexing in this field than in many others because religion, by definition, deals in matters that are deemed to reflect a higher, and perhaps more universal, truth than anything deriving from mere human society and its cultures. As such, a book devoted to the specific issues that concern religious professionals in a culturally diverse society would seem to be very much in order. Although the beliefs and practices that form the core of a faith community are not subject to negotiation or relativistic interpretation, we must remember that those beliefs and practices are taught and shared in groups of real people, whose social and cultural status is an integral part of who they are, how they learn, and what they aspire to. The need to understand and deal with cultural diversity is most acute when it comes to that form of religious activity collectively referred to as the "overseas missions." But because every community even within our own country is culturally diverse in ways that will be explored at length in following chapters, religious professionals working close to home will find many of the same principles relevant—and the need to study them perhaps even greater because they are so easy to overlook when they come clothed in the everyday and familiar.

Before we proceed, a few words of definition and explanation are in order. First and foremost, this book is addressed to Christians, primarily in the United States. In and of itself, the term *Christian* represents a huge diversity of denominations, sects, and faith traditions in the United States alone, and we would be ill advised to ignore the historical, social, and other forces that have led to and sustained that diversity over the centuries. Nevertheless, Christians of all types share certain values and core beliefs, elements of which, to be sure, are found among adherents of other religions (or even among people of no particular religious affiliation), but which, taken as a package, form a distinctive orientation.[1] I am confident that professionals working in Jewish, Muslim, Hindu, Buddhist, and other non-Christian faith traditions will find much in this book that is applicable to their situations, insofar as they encompass congregations that are internally diverse (consider, for one example, the large number of distinct national cultures likely to be represented in a typical American urban Islamic mosque) and have educational and social service outreach programs that put them in touch with many other segments of American society.[2] I am similarly confident that religious professionals, Christian or other, working in societies outside the United States will see numerous and, I hope, instructive parallels to their own situations. My rationale for addressing Christians in the United States is not therefore a matter of thinking that our situation is unique or somehow more important—it is simply a way of focusing the discussion. Trying to encompass all possible varieties of experience would lead to a book so generic that it would turn out to be yet another abstract text on "social problems" and would have very limited practical application. I do hope, however, that the book serves as an example for those interested in these issues in other faith traditions, who will develop training materials more specific to their own communities.

Second, when I speak of "religious professionals," I do not mean solely the ordained clergy. The fact is that in most contemporary Christian denominations in the United States, laypeople play a highly visible—sometimes even decisive—role in setting policy and carrying out the initiatives of their respective faiths. I recognize that many of those laypeople are, technically speaking, volunteers rather than professionals. But I will use the term *professional* to cover all those who work for the furtherance of the spiritual, educational, and social service missions of their faiths. On occasion, and mainly for the sake of stylistic variety, I use the terms *ministry* or *pastoral work* to describe these activities. Both of these terms are increasingly common generic ways of describing the work of both ordained clergy and laypeople although I realize that in some circles *ministry* is still restricted to the ordained clergy and *pastoral* pertains only to certain members of the clergy who hold designated leadership positions. I trust that no misunderstanding will arise from my more open-ended use of those terms.

Third, I realize that when I speak of Christians who work as religious professionals, I am most often referring either directly or by implication to those affiliated with a parish or other localized congregation. But I want to make it clear at the outset that my remarks are not limited by that context. In fact, the material in the book is fully applicable to those Christian religious professionals who work as chaplains in hospitals or the military or on college campuses, or who are members of vowed orders, none of which is a *parish* or *congregation* in the conventional sense of those terms. The emphasis is on any Christian religious professionals who serve a culturally diverse population, however that population is identified or defined. I will, on occasion, use the term *church* to refer to that population, again referring to C. S. Lewis, who prefers to speak of "the church," not as a specific local entity but as any functional "body of practicing Christians."[3]

Fourth, while there is considerable confusion and overlapping of terminology with regard to the phenomenon that is at the center of discussion in this book, I will use the following arbitrary distinctions just so that our discussion here can be clear. For one thing, I try to avoid the term *cultural pluralism*, because it most properly refers to a situation in which groups of diverse cultures coexist in a social space but do not really impinge on each other. I prefer to speak most generally of *cultural diversity*, which I define as a situation in which differences are recognized—even honored—but in which communication across the borders is considered necessary and beneficial. I restrict use of the term *multiculturalism* to a specific social and political movement that is often conflated with the "identity politics" of this or that minority group as against a perceived Eurocentric domination of educational and social institutions.[4] I would like to steer clear of the strictly political controversies engendered by contested meanings of multiculturalism, but I do want to state unambiguously at the outset that I *am* willing to argue from a bias in favor of cultural diversity as I have defined it in this paragraph—a position which I believe to derive from essential Christian principles, in addition to other reasons for supporting it. I am therefore, by implication, addressing those religious professionals who also recognize the value of learning about other cultures so that they can build bridges across the perceived divides in the interest of promoting their faith vision in the most socially effective ways possible.

I share with the cultural anthropologist DeWight Middleton the following core argument:

> [A]ll humans are essentially the same and share the same basic capacity for thinking and feeling as well as for social and moral reasoning. This general capacity takes specific cultural shape as particular groups of humans endeavor to survive in different environments and historical situations. A critically important part of human efforts to fashion a living . . . is to construct over time a cultural tradition, a continuing set of shared customs, knowledge, and beliefs that helps them to reach their goals. . . . Because each of us is emotionally and habitually committed to a tradition, we find it difficult to break its bounds. But we can, with earnest and informed effort, weaken our tradition's constraints sufficiently to come to know a different way of life.[5]

This workbook is offered as a means to give some pragmatic guidance to those Christian religious professionals committed to that "earnest and informed effort" to bridge the cultural divides that weaken our ability to work toward common goals.

1

BACKGROUND ISSUES

In Matthew's Gospel, Jesus' last meeting with his disciples in Galilee climaxes with an amazing proclamation: "All power in heaven and earth has been given to me" (Mt. 28:18). That universal power is to be handed down to them in turn, for he gives them a great commission: "Go, therefore, and make disciples of all nations, baptizing them in the name of the Father, and the Son, and of the Holy Spirit, teaching them to observe all that I have commanded you" (Mt. 28:19). The Christian movement may thus be said to have begun with an understanding that the salvation brought about by Christ was meant for all humankind and that the body of the faithful was to include not only people from all walks of life in Palestine, but from all the different parts of the world. The terminology was different in the days of the evangelists, of course, but it is not unfair to say that Jesus commanded his disciples to make disciples in turn of people of different cultures. This was the same Jesus, after all, who had reached out to Samaritans, Romans, and Syrophoenicians and conveyed the message of faith in ways that made sense to them. While faith speaks with one voice, the many different peoples of the world express themselves through a wide diversity of languages and customs. It is neither feasible nor desirable (nor truly Christian) to bulldoze away those cultural differences in order to make way for the faith, for people stripped of their distinctive cultural heritage are no longer fully human.

We see in the missionary journeys of Paul, for example, a pragmatic respect for different cultures. Paul's letter to the Romans (a group of Christianized Jews) is quite different in tone and style from the letter to the Galatians (a people who had gone from pagan to Christian without an intermediate Jewish step and who were apparently deeply confused about whether they had missed something). It is also very different from his address to the learned philosophers of Athens as reported in the seventeenth chapter of Acts. Paul's underlying theology remains constant, but he tailored his approach with careful attention to the customs and attitudes of the various people he encountered. Indeed, the basis of his overall strategy of evangelization was his profound insight that it was not necessary to adopt Palestinian Jewish *culture* in order to accept the message of Christ, even though the latter had first appeared in the context of that culture. So long as fundamental principles were not tampered with, Paul seems to have been quite willing to "do in Rome as the Romans do"—for example, allowing for the full participation, even leadership, of women in communities where such practices were culturally tolerated while advocating a more retiring role for women in communities with more patriarchal values, or advocating in general for an adherence to the lawful institutions of government so that Christians could go about their business without arousing undue suspicion or hostility. As Paul explains (1 Cor. 9:19–23):

> Although I am not bound to anyone, I made myself the slave of all so as to win over as many as possible. I became like a Jew to the Jews in order to win the Jews. To those bound by the law I became like one who is bound (although in fact I am not bound by it), that I might win those bound by the law. To those not subject to the law I became like one not subject to it (not that I am free from the law of God, for I am subject to the law of Christ), that I might win those not subject to the law. To the weak I became a weak person with a view to winning the weak. I have made myself all things to all men in order to save at least some of them. In fact, I do all that I do for the sake of the gospel in the hope of having a share in its blessings.

Paul concludes that section of the letter (1 Cor. 12) by drawing an analogy between the church and the body. The various parts of the body all work together for the common good, although they do not lose their own identities and distinct functions. And so Paul's approach of calling for personal conversion without necessarily condemning the social and cultural contexts in which individual Christians had to function was responsible in no small measure for the success of the Christian movement as it spread throughout the Roman Empire, and then beyond. The conversion of the European barbarians during the Middle Ages was accomplished in part through the expedient of incorporating various elements of pagan belief and practice into the Christian message (e.g., the celebration of the birth of Jesus, a date unspecified in Scripture, was assigned to the period of the Winter Solstice festival of pagan northern Europe, and many of the ritual trappings of that festival such as decorated trees, burning logs, and mistletoe have become universal symbols of Christmas). Over the centuries, mission-aries representing various Christian faith traditions have done otherwise—act-ing, in effect, on the maxim, "When in Africa (or Asia or the Pacific Islands, etc.) do as the Africans (or the Asians or the Islanders, etc.) do." But the most endur-ing missionary successes have come when Christian beliefs have found ways to accommodate the peoples' cultural practices (e.g., styles of music, tastes in deco-rating worship space, methods of reading and proclaiming Scripture).

Human cultures provide us with ways of thinking about and evaluating our material, emotional, and spiritual condition. They supply the symbols through which we give concrete expression to abstract ideas. They give us the means to extract a living from the natural environment. They suggest models for the proper behavior of both individuals and groups. Cultures, therefore, are neither optional nor interchangeable. Each culture is a distinctive pattern of actions and meanings. In short, a culture is a way of learning about and knowing the world. While the core of the Christian message is clearly universal, it must always be transmitted through the ways in which people come to know and understand. The kingdom proclaimed by the Gospel is lived by diverse people who are pro-foundly linked to their particular cultures, and so the building up of the king-dom cannot avoid borrowing the elements of human cultures.

When we evangelize through and with culture in all its diversity—rather than in opposition to it—we are practicing the "inculturation" of the Gospel. Through the process of inculturation, evangelizers transmit their own Christian values, but also take into account the good elements that already exist in other cultures and use them to further the Christian message.

As we move into a new millennium, Christianity—formerly the special pre-serve of Euro-American culture—faces the challenge of an increasingly diverse global population brought into ever closer contact by new transportation and communications technology. But an awareness of and appreciation for cultural diversity is no longer the concern only of those involved in the missions in far-away places. The United States in particular, always a tapestry of diverse cul-tures, is becoming increasingly heterogeneous. The prospect of dealing effec-tively with the cultural diversity in our own communities may seem daunting because it is so often couched in the rhetoric of political confrontation, but the richness that an appreciation of cultural diversity can bring to the faith is a gift worth striving for, in spite of the difficulties.

What might a Christianity sensitive to cultural diversity be like? We might surmise that at the very least it should strive for a recognition of diversity, a re-spect for cultural difference, and a healthy interaction between cultures—all without losing the fundamental message of the Gospel. These goals are easier stated than accomplished, of course. Those engaged in practical ministerial and pastoral tasks—whether they are ordained clergy or laypeople—will want to know how to go beyond the abstract, theoretical slogans and deal in a positive way with the diversity of the real communities in which they serve. It is a fundamental principle of this book that cultural diversity itself is not a problem. But we must recognize that groups are most often moved to learn about and respond to diversity when they *perceive* a problem in communicating across cultural lines.

One issue of immediate concern is the concept of "culture" itself. The fact is that *culture* is not just an all-purpose contemporary buzzword; it is a technical term that, if used in ways suggested by social scientists, might point the way to a more reasoned approach to the perceived problems of diversity. Father Gary Riebe-Estrella, a professor of cross-cultural ministries at the Chicago Theological Union, has put the case very clearly:

> Learning how to cross into someone else's cultural world first requires some understanding of the dynamics of culture in general, and, only then, the particular contours of [specific cultures]. Often too much attention is given to the specifics of individual cultural groups and almost none to helping people understand how culture works. As a result, when I see behavior among [a certain ethnic group] that I didn't learn about in the last workshop I attended, I have no way of understanding what that behavior means.[1]

I hope this workbook can contribute to the solution of this problem. I am a social scientist with a doctorate in cultural anthropology and nearly three decades of experience in the field. I have also earned a graduate degree in pastoral theology and have therefore been trying to put what I know as a social scientist about human culture to the service of the kinds of problems that confront both clergy and laypeople who work in ministry. One result of that endeavor has been a series of workshops designed to assist such people as they add an informed cultural dimension to their approach to common pastoral problems. Participants in those workshops have told me on many occasions that they would appreciate a resource that they could take back to their own communities to help them organize discussions about local issues. This workbook is a response to that expressed need.

My approach to cultural diversity differs significantly from those that equate "culture" exclusively with groups of different races or ethnic backgrounds. It is not always the case that a community includes people of different racial or ethnic backgrounds, but in my view culture is itself a diverse phenomenon; there are issues of cultural diversity even within the most apparently homogeneous group.[2] Being sensitive to people who are obviously different from us is, in many ways, the easiest part of the challenge, if only because it is usually very clear that there is a gap to be bridged. It is much more difficult to do as the Lord did and meet people where they are when on the surface they seem just like us and we don't quite understand that "where they are" isn't necessarily where "we" are.

As implied by the term *workbook*, this volume is by no means offered as a complete scholarly text in either social science or pastoral theology. Rather, it is intended to provide basic, usable information about some key concepts and how they can be applied. Although there is a reference section to direct the interested reader to more formal works dealing with these matters, the emphasis here is on material that can be immediately useful in everyday situations.

The core of the book is a series of case studies that demonstrate the ways in which an understanding of culture can help us address everyday issues raised by diversity. Pastoral decisions must necessarily involve reflection that is informed by faith as well as our experience of the world in which we live. This book is designed to provide some insights to help make the best use of what we know about our society—insights that enrich, but do not replace reflections of a more theological nature. It is my hope that we can go beyond the simplifications, stereotypes, and clichés about society and culture and come to grips with what is actually known.

It is important to remember that the aim of the case study discussions is for each group to come to some conclusions that are relevant to its particular circumstances. Raising awareness about the various factors that constitute cultural diversity does not mean that every religious community will want or be able to end up in a place where every conceivable difference is tolerated. Some forms of difference are simply incompatible with certain aspects of the teachings of one faith tradition or another. But it is, I believe, absolutely necessary for us to be as clear as possible about what is involved in cultural diversity so that we can make an informed decision consonant with our faith values, and not simply respond out of unreflective "conventional wisdom."

The case studies are all drawn from my own experiences in ministry in Catholic contexts, as well as from the experiences of people (of many different Christian faith traditions) who have participated in my workshops. Details have been modified to make the situations as applicable as possible across denominational lines, although the basic issues are ones that have come up with some frequency in the lives of people working in pastoral/ministerial contexts in our own society. These case studies do not provide final, authoritative answers; rather, they suggest a framework for discussion to guide local groups in their own reflections on their own particular problems as seen through the lens of their own particular faith tradition's perspective on the common Christian message. It is my assumption that while there is no one-size-fits-all answer, we can make effective use of a shared method and body of concepts to come to conclusions that speak to the particular pastoral concerns of our own groups. That result is, I believe, a reflection of the healthy diversity of contemporary Christianity at its best.[3]

The workshops on which this workbook is based have been delivered to groups of religious professionals, including religious educators, liturgists, campus ministers, youth ministers, social outreach workers, administrators, and members of religious communities; the vast majority of participants have been laypeople. I hope that the book will be of similar value to groups of professionals working in local church communities. It should also be useful in seminaries or other training facilities for the formation of those seeking ordination. I hope that the workbook allows groups in any of these environments to structure meaningful discussions tailored to their own local concerns. It is assumed that the discussion groups that will form to consider these matters will themselves be representative of the diversity of the community under study. It would be regrettable if we ended up fostering more processes in which "we" plan for "them." It would be a good idea, however, to review the material in the following chapters before putting such a heterogeneous group together, since it would be important to anticipate some of the issues (I will not stigmatize them by calling them "problems") that could be raised when people of diverse social and cultural backgrounds try to communicate with one another. After setting out some of the basic principles of cultural analysis, and then applying these principles to current conditions in the United States, I will offer some ideas about communicating across lines of perceived cultural difference so as to facilitate the group discussions keyed to the case studies that form the core of this workbook. Each of these segments of the book concludes with a set of questions. Some of these questions are tailored for individual reflection as a reader prepares to participate in a discussion group. Others deal with matters that could usefully be shared with the group as a whole. Some of them involve doing a bit of research and/or role-playing as ways of approaching the process of group discussion.

In short, it is not advisable to plunge directly into discussion of the case studies. Preparation on both the individual and the group levels is an important prerequisite to the stimulation of fruitful discussion of the specific issues.

2

CULTURE IN SOCIAL SCIENCE PERSPECTIVE

Culture: The Basic Concept

It would be convenient if there were a single, universally accepted definition of *culture*, but in fact there are many of them.[1] For our purposes, however, I will use a slightly modified version of the classic definition suggested by Sir Edward Tylor in 1871: "Culture is that complex whole, consisting of everything that a people makes, does, and thinks about, all of which they learn in the context of society." This definition has the great virtue of highlighting the three core elements that virtually all other definitions contain, regardless of the elaborations they may add around the edges.[2]

Tylor's definition stresses the *integrated* nature of culture, which is not simply a list of randomly assorted traits and characteristics, but is an organized system. That system encompasses a people's material production, its interpersonal interactions, and its ideologies or beliefs. Because it is a system, it is not easily broken apart. If it becomes necessary to intervene in a culture so as to modify some of its elements (e.g., introducing Christianity to a foreign people or introducing a set of new hymns to a congregation that has "always" sung something else) it is important to remember that a change in one part of the system can mean unintended changes in other, related parts. It is also unwise to take one element of a culture out of context and assume that it represents the whole (as, for example, assuming that permitting Spanish-speaking members of a congregation to select one Spanish hymn for the Sunday service completely solves the issue of paying due respect to Hispanic culture).

Moreover, culture is *learned*. There is still considerable debate over how much of human behavior is genetically patterned and how much is learned, but almost all social scientists at the moment would agree that learning ("nurture") is relatively more influential than biology ("nature"). Even things that *are* genetically patterned (such as our biological sex) are expressed behaviorally by means learned in a cultural setting. A biological female learns to be the sort of woman her culture expects, and different cultures expect different things of their women.

It stands to reason that something that has been learned can also be relearned, or learned in a new way, or even completely unlearned. We should never make the mistake of assuming that just because a certain behavior is "determined by culture" we are therefore stuck with it even when it becomes irrelevant, or even dysfunctional. After all, a piece of behavior may have meant something in its traditional setting (e.g., a woman in India marrying a man selected by her parents), but need not continue to have much meaning when the situation changes (as, for example, when that woman comes to the United States and lives among people who think it is very important to choose one's own mate). But while the *content* of what people learn can be nearly infinite in variety, the *form* in which they learn it, being more tightly integrated into the larger system of culture, is much more difficult to modify. For example, middle-class Americans prefer to learn through open discussion and do not do well with rote memorization; but the latter is the long-ingrained style of preference in many of the world's cultures that

CULTURE

1. INTEGRATED
   A. MATERIAL PRODUCTION
   B. INTERPERSONAL INTERACTION
   C. IDEOLOGY
2. LEARNED
3. SHARED IN NETWORKS DEFINED BY
   A. RACE
   B. ETHNICITY
   C. GENDER
   D. SOCIOECONOMIC CLASS
   E. SEXUAL ORIENTATION
   F. AGE
   G. DISABILITY

have a more vibrant oral tradition than ours. We should not assume that the style of learning that works for us must necessarily work for everyone else, or that resistance to the form in which a particular Christian doctrine is taught is the same thing as a rejection of the doctrine itself.

Another important aspect of the learning of culture is an appreciation for culture as a system based on *symbols*. Sometimes in everyday usage, the term *symbol* implies that something is unreal, or a second-hand substitute for something greater. But for social scientists, a symbol is anything verbal or nonverbal that comes to stand for something else, particularly when there is no obvious, natural, or necessary connection between the two. A flag is simply a piece of cloth with an arbitrary design, and yet it embodies all the many abstract ideas associated with the nation as a whole. All human societies use symbols to create and maintain culture. The fact is that we learn everything through the medium of language, and human language (unlike the call system of other primates) is almost entirely symbolic, in that the sounds and groups of sounds that convey meaning have no obvious, natural, or necessary connection to the things they are expressing.

Finally, culture is *shared* in the context of organized social groups, which are not unitary entities, but networks of relationships based on such factors as race, ethnicity, gender, socioeconomic class, age, condition of "disability," and sexual orientation. As such, we must guard against mistaking "ideal" culture for "real" culture—that is, assuming that what people tell us about what they are "supposed to do" is what they actually do. Ideal culture tends to be homogenized; real culture is the more accurate reflection of the diversity of the society. It is therefore wise to probe for *both* the real and the ideal. The greater the distance between the two, the more stressed by change the culture is likely to be, and the more sensitive people will be about the forces leading them to change. It is also important to remember that general patterns cannot be inferred from a single source, no matter how apparently knowledgeable, or how much of a leader that person seems to be. We must make sure that what such a person reports really is shared across the community and not just his or her personal axe to grind. People who present themselves as spokespeople for their communities are, in the experience of researchers, the ones with the most marked agendas. That this is so does not necessarily mean that such people are "wrong"—but it does mean that we must be prepared to verify their comments with other members of the group. In a similar way, we must be skeptical of anecdotal reports. Analyses based on more structured forms of social research are preferable to accounts of random personal encounters, although the latter can be very useful *if* enough of them are collected and a discernible pattern emerges.

It is extremely important to keep in mind that culture applies to all people. We sometimes have a tendency to think that culture is what exotic or nonmainstream people have, whereas what we have is just normal, reasonable behavior.

Therefore, the perceived problems posed by cultural diversity are not restricted to encounters between Westerners and people from faraway places; even a seemingly "average" American congregation or community can be marked by cultural diversity once we understand the underlying aspects of cultural differentiation.

What Cultural Analysis Tells Us About . . .

Race and Racism

Race is now regarded by most human geneticists as a culturally determined classification of people derived from accepted (and often stereotyped) ways of observing and evaluating heritable physical characteristics. Racism is a social practice of withholding civil and human rights from some people on the basis of presumed race. In the United States, most overtly racist laws have been removed from the books, but old attitudes are slower to change.[3]

It is certainly true that there are genetically based physical differences among people. Earlier generations of human biologists explained this phenomenon by assuming that "in the beginning" there were a few pure racial stocks (usually labeled "Caucasoid," "Mongoloid," and "Negroid"), although some mixing occurred over the course of time. Since it was European scientists who developed this model, it is no surprise that "Caucasians" came to the conclusion that they were the only remaining pure stock, and that others were "impure" or "mongrel" types who could be ill treated at will. But we now know that the human species has been genetically very mixed almost from the beginning and that the search for "racial purity" is a sham. Race is a cultural classification designed to deal with social problems, not a scientific classification with biological underpinnings. For example, the typical "racial" characteristics of skin color, hair tex-

---

PERSPECTIVE ON RACE

1. HUMAN SPECIES IS GENETICALLY DIVERSE
   A. THERE ARE NO PURE "STOCKS."
2. RACISM IS A PRODUCT OF LEARNED CULTURE, NOT OF BIOLOGY.
3. THERE IS NO CONNECTION BETWEEN RACE AND INTELLIGENCE.
   A. THERE IS NO CONNECTION BETWEEN RACE AND MORALITY.

ture, or configuration of nose and lips are all governed by a complex mix of genes, not by a single "racial" gene. And each of these genes is inherited independently of the others, so that it is possible to find a continuous gradation of these physical traits in every human population. The arbitrary drawing of lines between the physical characteristics of one group and its neighbors is a reflection of cultural (and hence learned) patterns, not of inbred, unchangeable biology. In fact, geneticists tell us that there is statistically more variation in physical types *within* the presumed racial "stocks" than there is *between* those "stocks."

Racism in the modern sense was largely a product of the European explorations in the Americas beginning in the fifteenth century. At first there was considerable debate in Europe as to whether the Native Americans even had souls—that is, whether they were even fully human. That debate was short-circuited when the "Indians" died off in huge numbers within the first hundred years after contact with Europeans. In need of labor to work fields and mines throughout the New World, the Europeans turned to Africa and to the institution of slavery. It was argued that enslaving black Africans was not really a sin since the Africans were of a manifestly different—and presumably inferior—racial "stock." Racism became both more virulent and more sophisticated in the latter part of the nineteenth century when various scholars began applying the principles of Darwinian fitness to the question of the competition among the races—a tactic that Darwin himself denounced. The tragic culmination of this "scientific racism" was the Nazi Holocaust.

The situation in the United States has been less lethal, but no less appalling in its consequences. For several hundred years our society functioned with institutionalized slavery that defined a cultural category (slaves) on the presumed basis of race. When the slaves were emancipated, they were not immediately welcomed into the white mainstream, and for many decades following the Civil War, American blacks formed a kind of pariah group, no longer enslaved in the legal sense, but certainly not free to participate fully in the society. The Civil Rights movement fostered considerable legal progress, but vestiges of the earlier pariah status still haunt many blacks today.

A recent wrinkle in the old American debate on race has concerned the supposed link between race and IQ. In its crudest form, this argument holds that blacks have inferior genes for basic intelligence, score poorly on standardized intelligence tests, and are thus unable to compete successfully for the high-paying professional positions that would lead to economic advancement. According to that scenario, crime, welfare dependency, and broken homes are all seen as artifacts of inherently low intelligence. The basic flaw in this argument is that IQ tests do not, and cannot, measure "intelligence" in the abstract. The most such tests can do is to measure an individual's ability to respond to certain culturally constructed categories of knowledge. People who begin with the handicap of being denied good education are unlikely to score well on such tests, not because they are inherently less intelligent, but because they have not been taught the socially learned skills required for responding to the specific kinds of knowledge represented on the tests. In effect, IQ tests measure only a fraction of the many different cognitive skills that actually make up the quality we call "intelligence." Given the complex nature of intelligence, it is highly unlikely that it can be attributed to a single gene, let alone that any cluster of genes could be specific to any one racial group (which, as noted previously, is not genetically "pure" to begin with).

Much the same argument can be advanced for "morality" or "character" as a factor of race. A complex quality such as morality cannot possibly be governed by a single gene (if, indeed, it is genetically based at all), nor can any supposed cluster of morality-related genes be specific to any given racial "stock." People of all levels of morality can be found in all groups, just as can people of all levels and kinds of intelligence.

Ethnicity and Ethnocentrism

Race is a culturally or socially constructed category based on presumed genetic differences. Ethnicity, by contrast, is a culturally or socially constructed category based on presumed social or cultural differences. Both are believed to represent social statuses that are ascribed (assigned at birth) and hence very difficult to change. In American popular mythology, a child born in a log cabin could grow up to become president (because political and economic power is achieved, not ascribed); but someone born "black" cannot become "white," regardless of his or her attainments, nor can someone born "Italian" literally become "Irish," no matter how much of the latter culture he or she learns.[4]

In the United States we inherit our ethnicity from our parents, although this process is no longer as clear as it once was, due to the increasing prevalence of intermarriage across old ethnic lines (and even across the racial divide). Recently, the celebrated young golfer Tiger Woods caused a stir by commenting on his mixed parentage. He has African American, Native American, and Asian ancestors and likes to claim affiliation with all of them. Some representatives of the several groups found in his family tree were incensed and demanded that he acknowledge himself to be one thing or the other. Mr. Woods, however, is probably more typical than his critics of coming trends. There is, for example, considerable support for adding a box for "mixed ancestry" or some such term to the standard racial and ethnic classifications on government forms. In the meantime, however, we must realize that traditional attitudes do linger and have consequences. Whatever his accomplishments, Tiger Woods would probably still have trouble hailing a cab in parts of some American cities because, despite his own disinclination to claim a primary affiliation, he is still widely perceived as "black."

Ethnic identification requires that the group in question see itself as distinctive and that this claim be recognized by outsiders. In the United States, people whose ancestry derives mainly from England rarely think of themselves as "ethnic" because elements of their traditional culture have for so long been the mainstream norm that they do not feel that claiming "Englishness" confers any special identity on them. The situation is different in Canada, however, where people of French heritage have a very strong alternative claim on the national identity; there, being English really is a matter of perceived distinctiveness. In Iceland, where virtually everyone is Icelandic, there is no point to speaking of Icelandic culture as an ethnicity; but a community of people from Iceland who have migrated to the heterogeneous United States might well want to invoke their ethnicity to the extent that they want to maintain the special identity of their group.

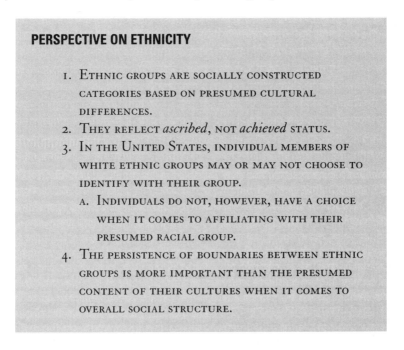

PERSPECTIVE ON ETHNICITY

1. ETHNIC GROUPS ARE SOCIALLY CONSTRUCTED CATEGORIES BASED ON PRESUMED CULTURAL DIFFERENCES.

2. THEY REFLECT *ascribed*, NOT *achieved* STATUS.

3. IN THE UNITED STATES, INDIVIDUAL MEMBERS OF WHITE ETHNIC GROUPS MAY OR MAY NOT CHOOSE TO IDENTIFY WITH THEIR GROUP.

   A. INDIVIDUALS DO NOT, HOWEVER, HAVE A CHOICE WHEN IT COMES TO AFFILIATING WITH THEIR PRESUMED RACIAL GROUP.

4. THE PERSISTENCE OF BOUNDARIES BETWEEN ETHNIC GROUPS IS MORE IMPORTANT THAN THE PRESUMED CONTENT OF THEIR CULTURES WHEN IT COMES TO OVERALL SOCIAL STRUCTURE.

Whereas race is a category usually imposed from the outside (typically, by those who are in the position of oppressors and applied to those whom they wish to oppress), ethnicity is often a self-chosen category, reflecting the interest of a group of people in preserving its identity. They may do so simply for reasons of communal pride, but they may also do so for very pragmatic reasons (e.g., in the United States, those who claim Native American ethnicity are eligible for various health and social service benefits not available to those belonging to other ethnic groups). The problem is that in a society as large and diverse as the United

States, the assertion of ethnicity is often more a matter of will than of observable behavior. The beliefs, behaviors, customs, and values of all ethnic groups tend to change and modify as one group encounters others. They do not necessarily blend into the same thing (as the old "melting pot" image led us to believe), but neither do they stay as they were when their ancestors first stepped off the boat from the "old country."

When I say that ethnicity is chosen, I do not mean that the "Italian" person becomes "Irish" simply because he or she wills it to be so. What I mean is that Italian and Irish Americans (and all the other "white ethnics" in the United States) can choose not to invoke any ethnic affiliation at all and simply disappear into the mainstream melting pot. This situation is clearly different from the way in which race is treated in this country—as noted previously, even a widely admired celebrity like Tiger Woods is not generally permitted to choose not to be African American in the eyes of the mainstream.

As such, the boundaries between ethnic categories are at least as important as the content of their cultures. Boundaries between ethnic groups may last through many historical and cultural changes. For example, the designation of "Indian" or "Native American" is one of vast complexity; everyone agrees that there are few, if any, genetically "pure" Indians left in the United States and Canada, and it is also clear that the thousands of quite separate native cultures that flourished prior to the coming of the Europeans have merged in many ways into a kind of blurred modern identity. But while there may be strenuous debate both popular and scholarly about "who is an Indian?" there is relatively little doubt that "Indian" and "Anglo" remain recognizable categories with a commonly recognized boundary.

Class

Americans fondly like to think that social class is one category of differentiation that they cast off with the Revolution.[5] An old, vestigially feudal society like England might have a class system, but not America, the land of opportunity. Americans simply do not like to talk about class, and almost all of them, when polled, self-identify as "middle class," a response that comes from both the plutocrat living in a mansion on the hill and the homeless person sleeping in a carton under the bridge. Americans also like to point out that we do not have a class system because individuals have a great deal of mobility—we are not tied to our ancestral group the way members of English social classes are presumed to be. In formal terms, *class*—unlike race or ethnicity—is in America an achieved rather than an ascribed status, but statistically speaking, most Americans are not as mobile as they like to think they are.[6]

PERSPECTIVE ON SOCIOECONOMIC CLASS

1. SOCIOECONOMIC CLASSES ARE THE RESULT OF *achieved* RATHER THAN *ascribed* STATUS.
2. THEY ARE DEFINED BY LIFESTYLE CHOICES.
3. THEY ARE RANKED BY SOCIAL CONVENTION, HENCE CRITERIA SHIFT AS THE VALUES OF THE SOCIETY CHANGE.
4. THEY ARE TIED TO POSSESSION AND USE OF MATERIAL PROPERTY.

In America we nonetheless have a system of ranking that is tied to material possessions. It is very important in the United States to drive the right kind of car, to live in the right kind of house in the right kind of neighborhood, to attend the right schools, to have the right kind of job, and so forth. But possessions are not the entire story; it is important to use one's possessions in the proper way. Flaunting one's wealth in a vulgar and ostentatious way is usually considered "low class" no matter how much of it one has. Newly rich computer moguls may be in better financial shape than certain "old money" families (who may even live in what is circumspectly referred to as "genteel poverty"), but we usually assign a higher class status to the latter. In sum, different classes exhibit and are partially defined by their own particular lifestyles. Lifestyle choices affect such diverse matters as ideas about child rearing, dating, food preferences, recreation, voting patterns, and religious affiliation. American class is therefore a system of ranked cultural traits. It may be an overstatement to call the situation a "system," since the numerous possible categories overlap considerably, but there are nonetheless definable, if often very subtle, criteria by which one American can "place" another on a ranked scale.[7]

Sex, Gender, Sexuality—and Sexism

Most cultures through time have understood there to be a very sharp distinction between male and female, and, like race, sex was assumed to be rooted in basic biology. But except for the fundamental and complementary roles assigned to males and females in the reproductive process—"sex" in its narrowest and most technical sense—we are once again dealing with a category that is more a cultural construction than a biological fact. Indeed, it is now common to use another term altogether, and to refer to the complex of behaviors and attitudes thought appropriate for males and females in a given culture as "gender" rather than "sex." The fact is that although almost every culture that we know of makes a distinction between male and female, their criteria for doing so vary widely. Complicating the matter is the question of sexuality, which is the specific set of behaviors determining how (or whether) one uses his or her sexual organs.[8]

It is a serious error to assume that *sex*, *gender*, and *sexuality* are just synonyms. In fact, confusing sex with gender leads to practices that keep people from achieving their full potential; this confusion has been particularly hard on women (e.g., girls who are good athletes but are told that it is not "ladylike" to compete in sports). Confusing gender with sexuality leads to injustices directed against gay men and lesbians and, indeed, leads to the stereotyping of everyone (in the sense that there is presumed to be only one "masculine" or "feminine" way to behave).[9] And confusing sexuality with reproductive sex has led to the negative stigmatization of all expressions of sexuality that do not lead to procreation.

The most widespread inequality in the modern world is that based on gender. Indeed, we may speak of "sexism" (or, more properly, "genderism") as the introduction of a power system to the disadvantage of one sex or the other, usually women. Some gender inequality is obvious and harsh: The burden of domestic violence falls disproportionately on women in most cultures, and, when there is a question of unequal pay for comparable work, it is almost always women who are shortchanged. But sexism is a more subtle problem than such cases might suggest. For example, the fact that work in almost every culture is divided into men's and women's spheres is not necessarily a problem. What *is* a problem is that the work of one group—almost always the men—is valued more highly than that of women. There are any number of possible explanations for why this is so, none of them completely satisfying. There may well be as many different reasons as there are different cultures. Nonetheless, the pervasiveness and persistence of this inequality is a fact of life that needs to be addressed.

One aspect of the division of labor that we should recognize in our own society is the relegation of women to a "second shift" of work. That is, many women not only work full-time for pay at jobs in the workplace; they also have the primary but unpaid responsibility for child care and housework. Women therefore work, on the average, fifteen hours a week more than men when these two "shifts" are combined. Even if they are fortunate enough to find employment in a field that compensates them equally with their male colleagues, they are still working what amounts to nearly an extra month of weekdays per year with no financial compensation. This is not to deny that there may be other (emotional, personal) compensation deriving from child care and housework, but, as noted previously, Americans do tend to equate personal worth with material wealth.

PERSPECTIVE ON MALE AND FEMALE

1. SEX IS A COMPLEX OF BIOLOGICAL TRAITS.
2. GENDER IS THE CULTURALLY SANCTIONED BEHAVIOR SPECIFIC TO EACH SEX.
3. SEXUALITY IS THE INDIVIDUAL (BUT CULTURALLY SANCTIONED) CHOICE ABOUT HOW ONE USES ONE'S BIOLOGICAL SEX TRAITS AND INTERPRETS HIS OR HER GENDER ROLE.
4. THERE IS A UNIVERSAL GENDER DIVISION OF LABOR.
   A. SEXISM IS THE DISCRIMINATORY INTERPRETATION OF THAT DIVISION OF LABOR.

There are different cultural ideas about gender inequality. American women assume that, as difficult as their situation can be, they are still better off than their counterparts in the Islamic world. But Muslim women often look with pity on Western women, who are treated with little respect, are denied the protection of the family unit, and who, by and large, do not work in sisterly cooperative groups.

One of the distinctive features of contemporary American society is the degree to which sexual orientation has become a factor in the political discourse on cultural diversity. While homoerotic feelings and homosexual tendencies probably exist in all societies, the existence of a gay *culture* is a relatively recent phenomenon. In some traditional societies, homosexual activities are ritualized and culturally sanctioned for certain people at certain times under certain circumstances; as such they help reinforce the general social order. But in modern society, such behavior is usually seen as "deviant." Nonetheless, the fact that people are now more willing to be open about their lifestyle choices means that organized groups can actively (and with some limited success) challenge social norms and definitions of deviance.

Age and Ageism

Aging is a natural process experienced by all of us, although the culture in which we live will have a significant say on how the process is interpreted and how we are treated by others.[10] Aging is, by definition, a lifelong process; but most cultures tend to set off arbitrary limits that determine socially sanctioned categories of "old age." In many traditional societies, those limits are either functional (e.g., defined by the inability of people to continue doing what other adults in the community do, such as men who must retire from hunting, or women who are past the childbearing years) or structural (i.e., defined by the assumption of certain social roles, such as becoming a grandparent or being asked to take a place on a council of elders). In our own society, the limits tend to be chronological (i.e., defined by the passage of certain birthdays, such as the legal age to apply for Social Security retirement benefits). The other main difference between urban, industrialized societies and more traditional folk societies is that ours has tended to "medicalize" old age—that is, we tend to see it as a form of disability that must be treated symptomatically (there being no "cure") rather than as a status that carries benefits of its own. Our popular culture promotes images of the "golden years," but it is no secret that most people, if given a choice, would opt out of the supposed serenity of those golden years in favor of the continued stress of young adulthood or even midlife. Ours is a culture in which "health" tends to be equated with "youth"; as a consequence, old age is popularly considered to be a detriment, and older people tend to join the ranks of those marginalized by our social system. The irony is that poor health is not as common among the elderly as we might assume; indeed, since older Americans tend to be both politically active and economically secure (relative to the general population), they have easier access to better health care than seniors did a generation ago.

This belief in the relative worthlessness of later life probably results from the success of our medical system, which has dramatically extended the life span from forty-seven to at least seventy years in little more than a few decades. In the not-too-distant past, people tended to die of acute illnesses when they were still in the prime of life; that there is now a very large group of people living far beyond that cut-off point, but with perceptibly declining faculties, is a kind of modern miracle—and yet it is a miracle that comes with a heavy social cost, given our general inability to incorporate this class into the prevailing "youth culture." Older people are viewed as a population that is essentially waiting to die, and while, statistically speaking, most older Americans do not spend a great deal of time in institutional care, it is important to remember that ours is a culture that considers institutional care a legitimate alternative to in-home family care—a situation that is not at all typical of more traditional societies. Institutionalized older people have been warehoused just as surely as people with chronic mental illness were a generation ago; treatment is preferentially given to those who have more of a chance of regaining a desirable quality of life. Even if they are not in nursing homes, the elderly do tend to be more socially isolated from their families than was the case a generation ago. According to U.S. Census statistics, approximately 30 percent of seniors lived with their families in 1950; by 1980, that rate had fallen dramatically to 9 percent. This trend certainly reflects the growing social isolation of the society in general—more people in all age groups live apart from their extended families. But the burdens of isolation bear most heavily on a semidependent population like the elderly.

There are also clear gender differences in the experience of aging. Although the gap is closing, men still have higher death rates at every age as compared with women. As a result, elderly women outnumber elderly men by a ratio of 3:2 (1994 statistics). These figures suggest that most elderly men are still married, whereas most elderly women are widows who live alone.

Social gerontologists once treated older people as a "quasi-minority" or as a "subculture." This approach has largely been abandoned, since it is clear that older people are and remain part of their culture—they do not suddenly become something altogether different upon reaching age sixty-five. This is not to say that there are not differences among the generations, for certainly older people will favor types of music or fashions that were popular in their youth, and they may espouse values that have gone out of style. They will have a distinct set of personalized referents, both sociopolitical (the War, the Depression) and popular (movies and radio programs) that are, at best, of only historical interest to younger people. But these factors really do not add up to a separate culture, minority or otherwise (and to speak of a subculture is inherently demeaning and should be avoided). Nevertheless, it is clear that as people age, they disengage from society, sometimes by preference (as in retiring and moving to a seniors residential complex), other times because of increasing physical or mental frailty. The question is how to promote healthy aging in the context of such disengagement.

PERSPECTIVE ON AGE

1. IN WESTERN CULTURE, AGE IS DEFINED BY ARBITRARY CHRONOLOGICAL CUT-OFF POINTS.

2. OUR SOCIETY HAS A TENDENCY TO MEDICALIZE OLD AGE—THAT IS, TO TREAT IT AS A HEALTH PROBLEM.

3. OUR SOCIETY HAS A TENDENCY TO MARGINALIZE OLDER PEOPLE, EVEN BEYOND THE LIMITED DISENGAGEMENT THAT OLDER PEOPLE MAY WANT FOR THEMSELVES.

4. HEALTHY AGING MEANS TAKING CHARGE OF THE PROCESS RATHER THAN BEING THE PASSIVE VICTIM OF IT.

One way to do so is to encourage a confrontational attitude in which older people take charge of their own aging and do not let society and its institutions dictate the process for them. Doing so has been said to involve five tasks: the acceptance of aging itself; the reorganization of one's "life space" in order to preserve an optimum level of control (e.g., moving into a small condo that can be efficiently maintained, as opposed to staying in a huge house that defeats the older person's best efforts to keep it up to standards); the substitution of alternative sources of need satisfaction (e.g., finding a widows' support group after the death of a spouse); the modification of one's basis for self-evaluation (i.e., taking stock of oneself in terms of what one *can* do instead of lamenting that which can no longer be done); and reintegration of values to evolve a new lifestyle (e.g., realize the value of conservation as opposed to acquisition and exploitation, of self-acceptance instead of self-aggrandizement, of being rather than doing, cooperation with rather than control of others).

Disability and Marginalization

Disability is most simply defined as a lack of or a limitation on competence. We usually think of it in contrast to some ideal or normative capacity to perform particular activities and assume that it prevents one from taking on a full role in one's society.[11] Disability is therefore something like sickness, except that the latter is temporary (ending either in recovery or death), while the former is often chronic. Disability, whether physical or mental, may be treated so as to rehabilitate the affected person; but it cannot (in theory, at least) be cured. Certain catastrophic conditions would be considered disabling in any context; but most of the conditions we think of as disabling are better thought of in relativistic terms. One is disabled relative to the standards of one's own society. For example, a person with mental retardation is quite seriously disabled in our society, because we place such an emphasis on technical skills, literacy, and the sorts of jobs that can only be accessed via advanced educational certification. But that same person might be able to function perfectly well in a society in which his or her manual labor might be highly valued, and where it would be possible to perform important and even prestigious social and economic roles that do not require intellectual acuity of the sort measured on standardized tests.

The United Nations declared 1981 the International Year of Disabled Persons, and beginning in 1983 it sponsored a Decade for Disabled Persons. These actions focused global attention on these issues and posed the question of how disability might be best understood in a world of diverse cultures. The key questions raised by the UN actions are as follows: How are deficits of the body and mind understood and dealt with in different societies? How is an individual's culturally defined identity as a person affected by disability? What processes of

PERSPECTIVE ON DISABILITY

1. *Disability* IS ALWAYS A RELATIVE, CONTEXTUALIZED TERM.
2. THERE IS USUALLY A PERCEIVED CONFLICT BETWEEN AN INDIVIDUAL'S CAPACITY AND SOCIETY'S DEFINITION OF THE GROUP TO WHICH HE OR SHE BELONGS ("ALL DEAF PEOPLE ARE . . .").
3. THERE IS AN INCREASING POLITICAL DISTINCTION TO BE MADE BETWEEN THE NEED FOR INDIVIDUAL EQUALITY AND THE DESIRE TO ASSERT THE RIGHTS OF THE DISABLED GROUP AS A WHOLE.

cultural change shape local perceptions of disability? One conclusion is already clear: Advances in medicine have made it possible for disabled persons to sustain themselves in the community, such that they no longer die quickly, nor do they need to be institutionalized. As a result, the interaction between disability and culture is now an everyday process.

In our culture, thinking about disability is colored by the value we place on equality. The word *handicap*, for example, originally referred to a kind of lottery game in which the winner paid a forfeit, an umpire holding the money in his hand in a cap. Later, the term came to be used to refer to games in which unequal competitors were weighted so as to make the match more equal. The word therefore has connotations of competition and efforts to create equality. In the same vein, disability suggests a loss of a needed competence, as opposed to *inability*, which implies an inherent absence of such a skill. The notion of loss is reinforced by the response of *rehabilitation*, which implies at least the partial restoration of a lost capacity. While we tend to think that the pursuit of equality is inherently noble, it does have a negative side: We tend to assume that society works better when differences are averaged out. This attitude makes some sense when the disability is something that society itself can do something about (like poverty or relative exposure to infectious disease), but it is problematic when it comes to conditions that are not, in the long run, amenable to homogenization. It is possible to "mainstream" children with disabilities in the school system, but doing so does not erase the differential skill levels. Indeed, groups of people with certain disabilities have recently begun taking strong political stands against the loss of their distinctiveness; some people with hearing impairments are very forceful advocates for the maintenance of a deaf lifestyle (some even call it a separate culture), promoting, for example, the use of sign language over lip reading or surgical implants.[12] Since American culture values individuality almost as much as it does equality, there is a very real conflict in our definition and treatment of people with disabilities: How do we balance the social call to treat them as much as possible like everyone else with the personal need of all humans to define their own special identity? It is generally the case that people with disabilities who live in small, face-to-face communities are given greater leeway to express their individuality, since their neighbors (many of whom are likely to be relatives or friends of long standing) are in a better position to put the disability into the context of the "whole person" whom they know and like. Those who live in large, complex, somewhat depersonalized societies, by contrast, are often treated categorically—it is no longer "Cousin Joe who's a little slow but helps out on his father's farm" but "He's mentally retarded and lives in that group home with others like him."

Perhaps affected by movements to secure rights for other marginalized groups, people with disabilities have been taking a much more active stance in recent years. Rights for disabled people have historically been advocated by family or professional caretakers, on the assumption that disabled people are unable to function effectively in the social or political arenas. But it is now common for advocacy to be conducted by the disabled people themselves. The *disabled* (and even the use of such a categorical term is now in dispute) can no longer simply be talked "to" or talked "about"—they must be talked "with."

Language

It is obvious that the people of the United States speak many different languages. Although English is still the national standard, there is considerable sentiment against declaring it the "official language." Indeed, school districts around the nation are instituting bilingual (or even multilingual) programs so that students who speak a language other than English at home can gradually ease into English-based instruction.[13]

In this section, however, I would like to focus on a slightly different issue, in keeping with the overall theme of this book, which is to look for cultural differentiation even within seemingly homogeneous mainstream society. When we speak of "bilingual education," there is a tacit assumption that English is a unitary standard. But the fact is that no language—and certainly not English globally and in the United States—is a homogeneous system in which everyone speaks like everyone else. One obvious factor that has long made for diversity within the English-speaking population of North America is regionalism. One need not be a trained linguist to spot the differences between a southern or a New England or a Canadian "accent." Regional "dialects" are probably being lost to some degree by the averaging forces of national media, but they are far from being mere relics of the past.

Whether or not we are bilingual, we all vary our speech dependent on the context. We subtly shift our vocabularies and even grammatical constructions depending on whether we are in a casual group of friends, giving a presentation to a business or school group, and so forth. We probably have specialized jargons that are useful when we are talking about sports, religion, politics, music, or other enthusiasms that we share with an "in-group" distinct from society at large. We probably modify our speech depending on whether we are talking to people of perceived different social status or to people of other generations.

A considerable body of literature, both scholarly and popular, has grown around the topic of gender differences in language. Several important trends have been identified. For example, women's speech tends to be more similar to the standard dialect than men's, women being more careful to avoid constructions that are considered to be "uneducated." By contrast, even highly educated men, such as politicians, sometimes adopt "low-class" speech patterns in certain contexts because they have connotations of hard labor and masculinity. In general, women's speech tends to reflect the historical lack of power accorded to women. A woman who has experienced a serious setback may say something like "Oh dear," or "Fudge!"—expressions that most men would use only satirically. (The popular writer Deborah Tannen invites us to read the lips of a football player who has just messed up an important play. Do we expect him to be saying, "Oh, my goodness!"?) By tradition, men's discourse is apt to be studded with locutions drawn from sports and the military, while women tend to elaborate on matters derived from fashion or style. Women have also been noted to share a tendency to end declarative sentences with an intonation more indicative of a question, probably another symptom of lesser power. These differences are being leveled just as surely as are those of the regional dialects, but vestiges of them persist.

Linguistic practices may be viewed as a form of "symbolic capital" that, with proper usage, can be transformed into economic and social capital. Any way of speaking has standing in a "linguistic market" to the extent that it provides access to desired positions in the labor market (and remember our previous discussion about the intimate relationship between class and economic gain). In rigidly stratified societies, even people who do not use the prestigious forms of speech recognize and accept its authority and correctness. The situation is considerably more fluid in the United States, of course, but I suspect that we all know that someone who speaks in an "illiterate" manner is highly unlikely to get to be the CEO of a Fortune 500 corporation, or get elected to the presidency, or become a bishop, no matter what other qualifications he or she may have. Culture being learned behavior, however, people can learn new ways of speaking so that they can fit into the positions they want to achieve.

PERSPECTIVE ON LANGUAGE

1. LINGUISTIC RELATIVITY:
   A. NO LANGUAGE HAS PURELY LINGUISTIC QUALITIES
      THAT CONFER DIFFERENTIAL ADVANTAGE, BUT
   B. LANGUAGES OR DIALECTS ARE SUBJECT TO SOCIAL
      EVALUATION.
2. LANGUAGES ARE FLEXIBLE AND CONSTANTLY
   CHANGING SYSTEMS.
3. SOCIOLINGUISTICS INVESTIGATES LANGUAGE IN ITS
   SOCIAL CONTEXT:
   A. GENDER
   B. CLASS
   C. RACE/ETHNICITY
4. STRATIFICATION MAY BE BASED ON THE ALLOCATION
   OF SYMBOLIC CAPITAL SUCH AS LANGUAGE USE.

Perhaps the most controversial example of linguistic diversity in the United States was the Ebonics resolution of 1996, when the Oakland, California, school board declared that many African American students did not speak Standard English but rather a distinct language called Ebonics, with roots in the Niger-Congo languages of western Africa. The case soon got caught up with the politics of funding for bilingual educational programs, although it should be kept in mind that the goal of the school board was mainly to permit the use of Ebonics to help certain students ease their way into Standard English–based instruction—not to set up an entirely separate curriculum taught exclusively in Ebonics. In any case, most linguists view Ebonics as a dialect (Black English Vernacular) rather than as a separate language, with its roots in southern English rather than in African languages. But classifying the vernacular as a dialect rather than a language does not demean it. In fact, Black English Vernacular is not an ungrammatical mess. It has its own regularities and rules of pronunciation, vocabulary, and syntax. As such, Black English Vernacular is not *linguistically* inferior to Standard English, although because it is associated with a poor racial minority group, it is almost entirely lacking in prestige in the wider society.

Family Background

When we think of the social context in which we learn our culture, we probably think first of the family, which we take to be the bedrock of our identity.[14]

We tend to have somewhat idealized and stereotyped views of family organization, assuming, for example, that the monogamous nuclear family is both the norm and the most desirable form of family. And yet we are becoming increasingly aware of the fact that "family" is a concept with multiple referents in contemporary society. Some forms of family that were once stigmatized (e.g., those headed by divorced women) are now almost too common to evoke much comment. Other forms (e.g., those composed of never-marrieds with children, or those formed by same-sex couples) are still considered somewhat deviant and may result in participants being shut out of some social benefits. But the fact is that the composition of U.S. households has been changing steadily and dramatically. Household composition is changing because more people leave home to work, often in different communities. Women are increasingly joining this labor migration; moreover, the increasing economic self-sufficiency of women makes it feasible for them to decide to delay (or even opt out of) marriage. Indeed, Americans seem to be both delaying and disvaluing marriage. The average age at first marriage for American women rose from 20.2 years in 1955 to 24.5 years in 1994 according to census figures. The comparable ages for men rose from 22.6 to 26.7. The number of currently divorced Americans quadrupled between 1970 and 1995, while single-parent families are increasing at a rapid rate.[15]

Statistics collected by the Current Population Survey of the Census Bureau may be summarized as follows[16]:

CHANGES IN U.S. FAMILY HOUSEHOLDS

	1970	1995
PERCENTAGE OF HOUSEHOLDS COMPOSED OF MARRIED COUPLES WITH CHILDREN	40%	25%
NUMBER OF PEOPLE PER HOUSEHOLD	3.14	2.65
PERCENTAGE OF HOUSEHOLDS WITH FIVE OR MORE PEOPLE	20%	10%
PERCENTAGE OF HOUSEHOLDS MADE UP OF SINGLE PERSONS	17%	25%

CHANGES IN U.S. FAMILY HOUSEHOLDS

	1970	1995
NUMBER OF FAMILIES MAINTAINED BY WOMEN WITH NO ADULT MALE HOUSEHOLD MEMBER PRESENT	56 MILLION	122 MILLION
NUMBER OF FAMILIES MAINTAINED BY MEN WITH NO ADULT FEMALE HOUSEHOLD MEMBER PRESENT	12 MILLION	32 MILLION
PERCENTAGE OF HOUSEHOLDS IN METROPOLITAN AREAS	67%	80%
PERCENTAGE OF FAMILIES WITH NO CHILDREN UNDER AGE 18 AT HOME	44%	51%

According to Bryson, "The increasing diversity of household types continues to challenge our efforts to measure and describe American society. The 'typical' household is an illusion."[17] For example, the nuclear family (married couple and their children) remains a cultural ideal for many Americans, yet such families comprise a scant 25 percent of the current population. There are as many single-person households as there are nuclear family households.

The maintenance of the prevailing consumer lifestyle means that in most cases all members of the household need cash employment. Work outside the home, however, puts obvious strains on family ties. There is an ironic side to this development: Parents who must work outside the home want to provide the best quality day care for their children. But such care is itself a substantial added expense, requiring even more attention to work. Child care has become an economic sector in its own right. Organized child care facilities accounted for 30 percent of all child care arrangements by the 1990s. Child care arrangements, however, vary widely according to the economic, regional, and ethnic characteristics of households. For example, children in families receiving public assistance were more likely to be cared for by relatives, as compared with other children while families in the South were most likely to choose organized child care facilities and least likely to choose relatives as primary care providers for their preschoolers.[18] Given the forces that work against the maintenance of the traditional family, responsible parents may become obsessed with using every last second of "quality" time to raise "successful" children, a quest that is both emotionally and financially draining in many cases.

These statistics suggest that "life may be growing increasingly lonely for many North Americans".[19] The mobility typical of an industrial economy seems to have precipitated the decline of extended families and descent groups by midcentury, but now in the postindustrial era, even nuclear families appear to be breaking up. The unmarried population of the United States rose from 28 percent to 39 percent of all adults between 1970 and 1993, and fully one-third of people sixty-five and older live alone. Many people seem to have replaced the traditional family with networks of friends, work, clubs, sports, and religion, but many others probably have not yet found an acceptable substitute.

Patterns of interaction with kin are one of the most important of the admittedly ambiguous markers of social class in the United States. For example, sharing with nonnuclear relatives is an important strategy that the urban poor use to adapt to poverty, while members of the middle and upper classes typically spend most of their time with nonrelatives (or, at most, with members of their immediate families). The lingering preference for the traditional family has led to the supposed crisis of teenage pregnancy, particularly when it occurs among people on welfare, although it is possible that it is the policies associated with welfare systems that created at least part of the "problem" in the first place. Moreover, although the African American family seems to be beset by single-parenthood, this status is not necessarily the emotional and economic dead end envisioned by middle-class analysts. Comprehensive statistical surveys conducted by the Institute of Social Research at the University of Michigan have demonstrated that families and churches are very important sources of emotional support and sustenance for African Americans.[20] Fully 20 percent of the black households in the survey were extended families, while 60 percent of respondents were in regular contact with relatives outside their household. Compared with the African Americans in the survey, many white Americans are cut off from their kin, living alone or in nuclear family homes in isolated suburban neighborhoods. Which group, then, represents the more salient social "problem"?

Family background is one of the most important reasons for the differentiation within a culture. Despite our stereotypes about the "typical American family," we can see from the preceding data that the contours of that family have been changing dramatically over time and that at present the situation is marked far more by diversity than by uniformity. It is by no means the case that nonnormative families are typical only of certain racial or ethnic or socioe-conomic class groups—the diversity spreads across the population. Nevertheless, there is still a tendency to define divergence from the supposed norm as "de-viance" rather than as positive "diversity." It is relatively easy for the mainstream to develop tolerance for racial, ethnic, class, disability, gender, or generational di-versity since these factors are no one's "fault"; it is relatively difficult to do so with regard to family structure when it, like sexual orientation gets caught up in moral evaluations of the right and wrong way to do things.

Power

Any political system—be it a civil authority such as a national or state gov-ernment, or an organized religious body—has two major tasks: the preservation (or, if need be, the restoration) of internal order; and the protection of the system from external threats. Both of these tasks depend on the quality and effective-ness of the cultural institutions available for controlling disputes. At one extreme is the system that is so controlled that no disputes whatsoever are allowed to sur-face (authoritarianism); at the other extreme is the society with no organized or institutionalized means to settle disputes (anarchy). Most societies, including the United States as a whole and the many independent secular and religious insti-tutions within it, fall somewhere in between. In the ideal, institutions for resolv-ing conflict are those that allow a society to leave room for discussion and that create and maintain a means to establish consensus and make orderly decisions. Every political system therefore has to find its own delicate balance between control and chaos; when two systems (classically, in the United States, "church" and "state") intersect, they must negotiate through their different ideologies about where to draw the boundary.[21]

Both church and state may be described as complex amalgamations of uni-centric and multicentric modes of political action. That is, both have mecha-nisms for discussion and debate, but then both strive to put on a unified face once a decision has been made. When two dissimilar political systems intersect in the civic arena, they have (in theory) the option of either ignoring each other or entering into open conflict with one another. Neither option is, for obvious reasons, desirable when the intersection involves church and state within the same society. How, then, is it possible for those operating primarily within one system (e.g., people in ministry whose first organizational identification is with the church side of the society) to find common ground with the state, which op-erates on the basis of different assumptions about power and conflict?

In the first place, although the American system is complex and dynamic, its form and substance ultimately derive from the Constitution and the presumed intentions of the framers of that document. Given the historical context of the framing of the Constitution, it is not surprising that the authors of the document were by and large more concerned with preventing tyranny than they were with facilitating the process of the freewheeling exchange of ideas. And so they built into the system the separation of powers dividing the three branches of government on the assumption that each branch would provide checks and balances on the others so that power was not allowed to accumulate in any one part of the system. In their zeal to avoid despotism, the framers were willing to tolerate a certain slowness—even stalemate—in the process of reaching a decision.

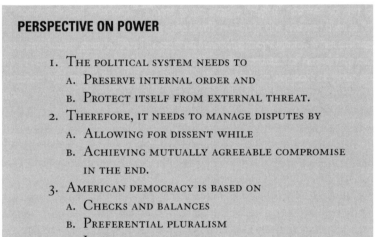

PERSPECTIVE ON POWER

1. THE POLITICAL SYSTEM NEEDS TO
   A. PRESERVE INTERNAL ORDER AND
   B. PROTECT ITSELF FROM EXTERNAL THREAT.
2. THEREFORE, IT NEEDS TO MANAGE DISPUTES BY
   A. ALLOWING FOR DISSENT WHILE
   B. ACHIEVING MUTUALLY AGREEABLE COMPROMISE
      IN THE END.
3. AMERICAN DEMOCRACY IS BASED ON
   A. CHECKS AND BALANCES
   B. PREFERENTIAL PLURALISM
   C. INCREMENTAL CHANGE.

But how does the average citizen gain access to the system in order to participate in the debate? At the risk of sounding cynical, we know that ours is a system of preferential pluralism—although everyone in theory can make his or her voice heard, in fact the ones who have a real voice are those people (or, more likely, those organized groups) that have the resources to put their representatives in office and influence representatives' deliberations once they are there. Since there are a number of such preferred groups, it becomes necessary for decisions to be reached through a process of bargaining and compromise; except in rare, nearly cataclysmic circumstances (e.g., the declaration of war), the resulting decisions are thus almost always incremental changes rather than sweeping reforms.

The point is that although Americans in theory are all equally empowered to participate in and influence the decision-making process, there is actually differential access to the system, which is usually more attuned to the attitudes of organized groups than to individuals. Moreover, the groups granted such preferred access are those with either financial or political clout (i.e., the resources to elect—or throw out—representatives). Affirmative action plans have made many formerly disempowered groups (e.g., women, minorities) players in this system, but even those with the most ambitiously progressive agendas usually end up becoming part of the process of incremental accommodation. But any institution or organization, even those that stand on the church side of the divide, must learn to adapt to that context of negotiation in order to make the best of American society.

Discussion

It should be clear from this chapter that culture is far more complicated than the simple list of superficial customs and traits that we use to stereotype groups might suggest. It should also be clear that my working premise in this book will be that while large categories exist (race, ethnicity) by which we differentiate one culture from another, there are even more categories (gender, socioeconomic class, age, disability) that create diversity even within a given culture. Cultural diversity awareness is therefore not only a matter of recognizing those who are superficially "other"; it is also a matter of recognizing how we maintain a sense of our own unity even in the face of numerous factors that make members of the same group different from one another.

The following questions are designed to aid you in applying these general principles to your own circumstances. It is recommended that you ponder these questions privately (perhaps keeping a running journal as your ideas grow and change during the process of working your way through this book), although you may also wish to share them with members of whatever groups are convened to discuss the case studies in the later chapters.

1. Think about your own culture. Draw a pie chart in which you apportion the various elements that make up *your* complex whole (e.g., x percent for religion, y percent for educational background, z percent for occupation, and so forth).
   a. Do you think that anyone else's pie chart would resemble yours? Since there will probably never be an exact match, how much similarity would you consider necessary for you to consider there to be a "close enough" resemblance?
   b. Can you think of a different diagram or model that better represents your idea of what culture is and how it works?
2. A popular book suggests that everything of value that we learn we learned as toddlers. Make a list of the things you learned "in kindergarten" that you still consider central to your *culture*, as opposed to your unique, individual personality.
   a. Make another list in which you include things you have learned in the years since kindergarten that you consider central to your culture.
   b. What, if any, differences do you notice in the amount, kind, or cultural saliency of things learned early in life as opposed to those acquired later?

3. Pretend that a cultural anthropologist or sociologist from another country has come to your town or neighborhood to study its culture. Would you be willing to serve as his/her informant? If so, why? If not, why not?
   a. If you do agree to serve, what would you tell the researcher if he/she asks what is most important in creating a sense of a cohesive culture in this geographically bounded space? By contrast, what factors make for diversity within that culture?
   b. If you do not want to serve, would you feel comfortable recommending someone else? Who? Why?
4. Do you consider yourself to belong to any particular race? If so, which one? Why?
   a. Do you categorize other people, either implicitly or explicitly, according to racial categories? (By *categorize* I do not mean "negatively stereotype." Answer "yes" to this question even if you have an extremely positive view of members of a certain racial group. Answer "no" only if you can honestly say that you treat every person as a unique individual on his or her personal merits without reference to his or her presumed affiliations.) If so, what criteria do you consider in making such categorizations? How many categories do you consider to be operative in your own social circle? What are they? How many do you think are operative in the world at large? What are they?
   b. What do you think are the pros and cons of seeing race as a "social construction" rather than as a biogenetic fact?
5. Do you consider yourself to be a member of an ethnic group? If so, which one, and why do you recognize that affiliation? If not, why not?
   a. If you see yourself as part of an ethnic group, what features do you consider most important in making your group distinct from others?
      i. On what occasions are you most inclined to emphasize your ethnic affiliation? When, by contrast, do you downplay it?
   b. If you do not see yourself as part of an ethnic group, do you recognize ethnic categories for others, and, if so, what are they and by what criteria are they defined? Or do you think the whole concept of ethnicity is irrelevant?
6. Come up with your own definition of "social class" (note: I do not say "socioeconomic class" since that might prejudice your response) as it pertains to the United States.
   a. According to your definition of social class, to which class do you belong? Is it the same or different from the one to which your parents belonged? Why?
7. To what extent is "class" in America (as you have defined it) governed by race and/or ethnicity? To what extent is racial or ethnic identification governed by class?
8. To which biological sex do you belong? What do you consider to be the *culturally* proper expression of your sex (i.e., what is the culture's definition of

your gender role)? To what extent to you conform to that role expectation? In what ways do you differ from it? Why? What are the consequences of your difference?

9. What cultural factors help us make personal decisions about our sexuality? What cultural factors might be seen as impediments to making informed and personally satisfying decisions about sexuality?

10. A popular book claims that "women are from Venus, men are from Mars," suggesting that there are essential and categorical differences between the sexes that spill over into culturally patterned gender behavior. Do you agree? Why? If not, why not? What has been your personal experience of communicating with someone of another gender? What were the positive aspects of such communication? What were some of the barriers?

11. In what aspects of our society, if any, do you think gender inequality is most marked? Why?

12. There are several different perspectives that may inform our view of aging including our own personal experience of moving through the life cycle; dealing with the aging of a loved one; working as a professional care giver. What are your own thoughts about aging? From what experiences do they spring?

    a. Which *cultural* factors facilitate positive aging in our society? Which ones impede it?

13. Several terms are often used interchangeably: the handicapped, the disabled, the differently abled, persons with handicaps, persons with disabilities, persons with different abilities, the physically/mentally challenged; persons with physical/mental challenges. Granted that they all refer to the same population (what linguists call the "common denotative meaning" of the terms), do you agree that they all convey the same thing (or what linguists call the "denotative meaning")? If not, how do you distinguish among them? What are the pros and cons of using one or the other in preference to the rest?

    a. Do you think that a new term might be more appropriate for referring to this population? Can you think of one? If so, explain and defend your choice.

14. How many different ways of speaking can you identify in your own linguistic patterns? In what contexts do you shift from one to the other?

15. Answer the following questions first based on what you have learned from the popular media and/or social science studies, and second, based on your own personal experiences.

    a. Do men raised by women get along better with women than do men raised by men or by a married couple?

    b. How does a girl form a female identity if she is raised by a man?

    c. What is the relationship between a parent's sexual orientation and a child's identity formation?

    d. Are African Americans closer to extended family kin than white Americans are?

16. Leaving aside legal and constitutional analysis, what *in your experience* is the main difference between the realm of "church" and that of "state" in the United States?

17. Group decision making may be authoritarian (made by a leader and carried out without discussion by the rest), hierarchical (a designated elite group discusses and reaches a conclusion that the others follow), or cooperative (full and equal participation by all members in the discussion). What style of decision making do you think is most typical of your primary reference group (as a religious professional)? Do you think it is the most effective method in that context? Why or why not?

    a. If a decision-making group is internally diverse (and, as our discussion here clearly suggests, it almost always will be), how might cooperative decision making be implemented? In other words, how can the special interests of segments of the group be balanced against the well-being of the group as a whole (e.g., simple majority rule, some system of checks and balances)?

18. On a scale of 1 to 5, rank your personal degree of comfort when dealing with someone who represents one of the following categories of people first in your capacity as a religious professional and second in your private life. (1 = very comfortable, 5 = very uncomfortable). When you have done so, see if you can find any patterns in your responses. If so, how can you account for them?

    a. Racial group

        i. Caucasian

        ii. African American

        iii. Asian

        iv. Native American

        v. Indeterminate or "mixed race"

    b. Ethnic group

        i. European-derived ethnic (e.g., Irish, Italian, Polish, German, etc.)

        ii. Non-European ethnic (e.g., Japanese, Chinese, Filipino, Arab)

        iii. Other religious/faith tradition

            • Christian of a denomination other than my own

            • Jewish

            • Muslim

            • Hindu

            • Buddhist

            • Atheist/agnostic

c. Social class
   i.   My own
   ii. Other, perceived as "higher" than my own
   iii. Other, perceived as "lower" than my own
d. Gender
   i.   Male
   ii. Female
   iii. Indeterminate
e. Generation
   i.   My own generation
   ii. The generation of my parents or older
   iii. The generation of my children or younger
f. Disability
   i.   Mobility challenged (e.g., person in wheelchair)
   ii. Other physical impairment (e.g., loss of limb)
   iii. Visual impairment
   iv. Hearing impairment
   v.   Mental illness
   vi. Mental retardation
g. Power
   i.   Group to which I belong in my decision-making community
   ii. Group with perceived greater power in my decision-making community
   iii. Group with perceived lesser power in my decision-making community

19. Of all the attitudes you have identified in this series of reflections, select three that you would most like to change. Identify at least three action steps for each of the selected attitudes that will help you accomplish the change. Don't think you need to make the change all at once—specify a time line for taking your steps toward change.

3

REFLECTIONS ON CULTURAL DIVERSITY

The experiences of those in ministry in a culturally diverse society need to be interpreted against the background of the society at large. Therefore, before we consider specific cases of diversity in ministry, let us take a quick overview of the issues surrounding diversity in the United States in general.

Modern social science tends to treat all purported measures or indices of difference as *social constructions*, rather than biological inevitabilities. But just because characteristics that make for difference are social and cultural rather than biological does not make them less "real." Indeed, the very real consequences of racism, sexism, ageism, class conflict, ethnic cleansing, and so forth compel us to deal with *perceived* interhuman differentiation.

To understand intergroup relations, we must recognize that almost all human groups are capable of looking on other groups as "strangers." While some cultures have historically counted it a point of honor to welcome strangers, it is more often the case that outsiders are considered inferior and are treated with distrust and even hostility. Aristotle was perhaps the first philosopher to turn his attention to this phenomenon, and his observation in *The Rhetoric* is still pertinent: "We like those who resemble us, and are engaged in the same pursuits." People perceive strangers primarily through categorical knowing—the classification of others on the basis of limited information obtained visually, and perhaps verbally. There is a tendency to confuse an individual's characteristics with those of the group ("All Italians sing beautifully"). The influential early twentieth century sociologist Georg Simmel suggested that strangers are both inside and outside—physically present and participating, but originating in another place, either a different geographic locality, or a different "psychic space" such as that presumably separating men and women. Alfred Schutz, a sociologist who was himself an immigrant to the United States, noted in a comment on Simmel's work that strangers also lack the insiders' understanding of the local jargon, customs, beliefs, symbols, and everyday behavior. As a result, they often act in a way that seems clumsy and tentative, which only emphasizes their strangeness.

The tendency to view the world in terms of insiders and outsiders is known as *ethnocentrism*, the belief that one's own group represents the best and most reasonable way of life, and that all other groups are ranked with reference to it (usually in a negative way). The assumption that "we" are better than "they" results in out-groups becoming objects of ridicule, contempt, hatred—or just blind indifference. Such attitudes lead quite naturally to stereotyping, prejudice, discrimination, even persecution.

There are three ways to understand patterns of cultural diversity in the United States. *Functionalist theory* is a belief in the stability and essential cooperativeness of the social system. Under ideal conditions, a society is in a state of balance, with all its parts working in harmony. When problems arise, it is because some parts of the system have become dysfunctional, often as a result of rapid social change. Changes in one part of the system require compensating adjustments elsewhere. Functionalists believe that all problems associated with diversity can be resolved through adjustments to the social system, returning it to a state of equilibrium through small corrections to an already harmonious society.

By contrast, *conflict theory* has been influenced by the Marxist image of an elite exploiting the masses, such that society is defined not by its stability, but by its disagreements, tensions, and intergroup clashes. Perceived differences almost always result in discrimination, as those in power seek to maintain their control by disvaluing those who express alternative behaviors and values.

Interactionist theory focuses on such small-scale behaviors as social distance when talking and the sharing of commonly understood terms, rather than on the larger social institutions that concern the functionalists and conflict theorists. Interactionists emphasize the shared symbols and definitions people use when communicating with one another. By means of symbols such as those of spoken language, gestures, body language, tone of voice, appearance, and popular culture images, people communicate, create impressions, and develop an understanding of the world. Interactionist theory sees diverse cultural groups as engaged in a set of negotiations or dialogues, rather than conflicts.

Culture provides the definitions by which members of a society perceive the world around them. Language and other forms of symbolic interaction provide the means through which this knowledge is perceived and transmitted. One becomes a member of a culture by learning both the language and the symbol system of the society. Moreover, unless that society is isolated from the rest of the world (highly unlikely, given modern modes of transportation and communication), it undergoes natural change through cultural contact and the diffusion of ideas, inventions, and practices. Within large societies, there are usually cultures that may be gradually assimilated (convergent cultures) or that may remain distinct (persistent cultures). In the United States, most of the so-called white ethnics (e.g., Irish, German, Italian, Polish) have become convergent cultures; members of such groups may choose to announce their ethnic affiliation for special occasions, but for the most part they can and do blend into the mainstream. African Americans, by contrast, are an example of a persistent culture since, in the United States, skin color is treated as the irreducible mark of one's social status; even black people who are, economically speaking, middle class, are still thought of and are treated like all other blacks.

Three theories of divergent group ("minority") integration have been prominent in American public policy. *Assimilation* was the dream of those who assumed that newer immigrants, or others of marginalized status, would have to take on (or, at least, assent to) the characteristics of the elite if they were to be tolerated. *Amalgamation* looked forward to the creation of a new breed of people with a distinct culture, "melted" out of the many origins in a common "pot." The assumption of both assimilationists and amalgamationists was that American society *should not* in the ideal be a culturally diverse one. But *accommodation* (or "pluralism") recognizes the persistence of diversity in a society even though there is a commonly shared core of culture. The past, present, and probably the future of the United States are all bound up in the word *diversity*. United by a core of culture and shared beliefs in certain ideals, the people of the United States have nonetheless not always understood their common bond or openly accepted one another as equals. In the terms developed in the preceding discussion, we remain a nation of strangers. Assimilation and pluralism continue to vie for prominence among policymakers and opinion leaders. Despite some progress, the United States has never fully resolved its race-relations question, and the legacy of American racism has been a widespread assumption that toleration of *any* difference is bound to lead to unmanageable stress in the social fabric. But it is important to remember that diversity has always been part of the American experience, and it has never really destroyed either the assimilation process or the cohesiveness of the society, despite popular perceptions to the contrary.

We all have a general awareness of the issues involved in living in a culturally diverse society, but several recent experiences have focused our attention on these matters. Some of these experiences deal specifically with race and/or ethnicity, the most commonly cited factors in cultural diversity, but others demonstrate that implicitly we have come to an appreciation of other factors making for a multicultural society.

For example, immigration reform has sparked debate across the United States. The problem, as seen by many Americans, is that the longstanding predominance of European immigrants is threatened by immigration from Latin America, Asia, and Africa. Proponents of restricted immigration are concerned about the ability of the United States to absorb large numbers of new immigrants. It is often pointed out that the great wave of European immigration coincided with the industrial expansion of the American economy at a time when there was still ample land in the West; neither of these conditions is still operative. One often hears fears of "losing American jobs" to newcomers, as well as concerns about the United States losing its historical character—changing from a largely white, English-speaking nation to a largely nonwhite, polyglot society. These fears are accentuated by the continuing relatively low birthrate among members of the white middle class; immigration is now perceived to account for a larger share of population growth than ever before. Immigrants are thought of as a drain on the increasingly stressed social service, health, and education systems. Economists have demonstrated that immigrants do not, in fact, take away "American jobs," and that they, in fact, contribute relatively more in taxes than they take away in social service expenses, but Americans remain apprehensive. Polls, for what they are worth, consistently reveal that between 65 and 75 percent of Americans claim that immigration is bad for the country. There is particular resentment directed against undocumented aliens who take jobs and are serviced by the health care, educational, and other systems in ways to which they are not legally entitled.

The changing nature of immigration has fueled the debate over bilingual education. Bilingual education programs can be either transitional (gradually phasing in English over a designated period of time) or maintenance (continual native-language instruction with the explicit goal of helping students preserve the heritage of their homelands). The former is a strategy favored by those who adopt an assimilationist policy, while the latter is supported by those who favor pluralism. It is often forgotten that *bi*lingual education means exactly that—the students are ultimately supposed to be literate and fluent in both English and their native language. The perception, however, is that such programs support the native languages at the expense of English, resulting in frequent calls to mandate "English-only" services and facilities. (It is ironic that most Americans seem to think the people of Québec are quaint and misguided in their "French-only" fervor.)

Controversies surrounding "new strangers" among us have entered our political discourse under the label of *multiculturalism*. When that term first entered the American public vocabulary in the 1970s, it meant the inclusion of material in the school curriculum that related the contributions of nonmainstream people to U.S. history. That piecemeal approach soon gave way to a more concerted effort to change all areas of the curriculum to reflect the diversity of U.S. society and to develop in students an awareness of and appreciation for the impact of the marginalized and disempowered elements of society. American history was not, it was pointed out, simply the record of triumphant European males. The intent of the multicultural movement was to promote an expanded American identity, one that recognized previously excluded groups as integral components of the whole.

The multiculturalism debate, however, has shifted in recent years away from an assimilationist tendency toward a more overtly pluralistic one. Latter-day multiculturalists reject the notion that formerly marginalized groups share more with each other (and with the "mainstream") than has previously been recognized. Indeed, the new emphasis is on "separatist pluralism"—the notion that these different groups are *essentially* different from one another in ways that make their integration into a common society not only unlikely but actually undesirable. The focus on separate group identities as opposed to a collective national identity is often taken as a threat by representatives of the erstwhile mainstream. To create a positive group identity, the new multiculturalists do more than advocate teaching and maintaining their own customs, values, and heritage. They also refuse to acknowledge the dominant culture's customs, values, and heritage. For example, Native Americans object to the celebration of Columbus Day as a national holiday, since in their view Columbus was no hero, but the herald and architect of the genocidal European takeover of the Americas.

The multicultural controversy does not only apply to racial and ethnic groups. Multiculturalists have also been active in calling into question the standard canon of studies in all the academic disciplines because it reflects the attitudes of white male elites. The voices of women, the poor, people with disabilities, those with variant sexual orientations have traditionally been suppressed by those who established the canon. Multiculturalists argue that a new approach to learning across the curriculum must include these other voices, much to the consternation of people who were educated in that canon and have a difficult time envisioning what an alternative curriculum would look like. It is, after all, a real challenge for most people, even the most open-minded, to learn something that may threaten their existing way of life.

By the 1990s, various liberation movements joined in a loosely structured coalition that is sometimes believed to stand behind the curse of political correctness. (It is one of the ironies of contemporary American life that it is considered an insult to accuse someone of being "correct.") Advocates of political correctness have sought to create in most of the major institutions of American society a tolerant atmosphere for all people. There are now established guidelines for proper speech and behavior that are aimed at eliminating practices that might be construed as hostile or threatening by nonmainstream people. Those distressed by the political correctness movement have sought refuge in the First Amendment protection of free speech, although advocates of "p.c." often accuse their critics of hiding behind the Constitution in order to preserve their own cultural and political domination.

It is therefore clear that in the political and social climate of contemporary America just about everyone is aware of the diversity of our culture; the problem is whether to deplore or celebrate that diversity. Controversy still surrounds the extent to which the institutions of American society (schools, churches, the ballot box) can or should be mobilized to promote groups' positions with regard to either the promotion or maintenance of diversity. A poll recently taken at the request of the Ford Foundation revealed this divided consciousness: An astonishing 71 percent of the respondents agreed that "our society is multicultural and the more we know about each other, the better we get along." At the same time, 60 percent claimed that "the nation is growing apart rather than together."

We can suggest the following general conclusions on the basis of this overview of American cultural diversity:

1. We are a "nation of strangers." Few societies are like us in having been constructed largely out of waves of immigration. Fewer societies still are like us in having enshrined a tolerance for different expressions in their national charter. Thus, despite the natural tendency toward tension whenever differentiated groups coexist in a single society, our national ideals seem to suggest that we honor our diversity. The old assimilationist "melting pot" is no longer an operative metaphor for our society.

2. All markers of differentiation—even those we conventionally attribute to inherent biological characteristics—are social constructions. They are learned and shared behaviors that have become institutionalized in our patterns of thinking and behavior. Although constructed rather than inherent, such differences cannot be merely swept away. We must take account of them, but understand the dynamics of culture that enable us to reconfigure that which we learn and share.

3. The committed Christian would seem to have a special mandate to enter into dialogue with culture. Dialogue is a two-way street that presupposes mutual respect and understanding; it is not take-it-or-leave-it preachment. This thrust is not a recent innovation, but seems implicit in the teachings and actions of Jesus and his followers. As St. Paul so forcefully argued, it was not necessary for potential converts to accept the constructions of Jewish culture (e.g., circumcision) in order for them to accept the Gospel, even though the Gospel message had originally been taught in the milieu of Jewish culture.

4. The culture with which Christians must dialogue is not a single, homogeneous entity, but a multifaceted, diverse conglomeration of demographic factors and group characteristics.

5. Racism may be considered the primal sin of American society, and there is still a tendency to see all social differentiation in the United States through the filter of race. But differentiation extends beyond the obvious categories of race and ethnicity and includes such factors as age, class, gender, conditions of disability, and sexual orientation. Our dialogue must encompass all these dimensions of social differentiation, not to melt them together, but to understand their diverse contributions to an overall American mosaic.

6. Engaging in this sort of dialogue between faith and culture requires a format that allows for the airing of divergent views, even as it demonstrates the tendency of culture to seek consensus.

7. Interactionist theories of social process, which focus on acts of behavior, are more workable in such a dialogic setting than functionalist or conflict theories, which emphasize institutional forces that may seem far beyond the capacity of local participants to affect.

Discussion

As in the previous chapter, it is a good idea to sort through your own ideas on the issues suggested in the workbook before you participate in a group discussion. Once again, I suggest that you keep a journal to track the development of your responses over the course of the process. You may or may not wish to share your responses with other members of the group that convenes to discuss the case studies.

For this chapter, you are to dialogue with each of the preceding seven general conclusions. Respond to my statements in terms of your own experiences (both personal and professional) rather than in terms of social science research that you have learned in this book or elsewhere (unless, of course, you are by profession a social scientist). How do you think your responses are shaped by your being a Christian? by your being a religious professional? How do you think those responses might differ from those of Christians not actively involved in ministry? from those of non-Christians?

4

THE UNITED STATES AS A PLURALISTIC SOCIETY

Even in colonial times, the territory that was to become the United States was home to people of diverse backgrounds. Nevertheless, the United States developed—and, for a very long time, continued to see itself—as a Christian nation, defining Christianity mainly in terms of the Protestant faith tradition. It is no longer possible to maintain this identity, given the size and prominence of non-Protestant Christian communities (e.g., Roman Catholic, Orthodox) as well as the increasing visibility of people of Jewish, Islamic, Hindu, and Buddhist affiliations—or of no formal affiliation at all. In former times, it was possible to think of religion in terms of both community norms and private faith. But modern America is a society in which most people think of religion in terms of individual beliefs and practices and are reluctant to admit its relevance in the public arena. Indeed, we often use the current situation of religious pluralism as the reason not to include religion in civic life—with so many different religions (including a generalized "spirituality" not associated with any organized religious body) out there, it is impossible to privilege one in a public event without potentially offending all the others.

Beginning in the 1940s, the Supreme Court developed an interpretation of the Fourteenth Amendment that prevented states from enacting laws establishing religion or preventing free exercise of religion. The Court emphasized the Jeffersonian "wall of separation" between church and state and has continued to rule that the government cannot favor one religion over another or "advance religion" in any way. Despite these tendencies, both law and public discourse continue to echo our past as a homogeneous Christian society. White House and Congressional meetings are convened with prayers, and while there is more evident diversity in those expressions than in former times, Christian forms still dominate. It is Christmas, not Hanukkah or Divali, that is the focus of public attention even by those professedly secular in outlook. Large, nondenominational Christian organizations such as Focus on the Family distribute Christian videos, books, newspaper columns, and radio programs on a national, even global, scale. Moreover, issues of school prayer, the posting of the Ten Commandments, the display of Nativity scenes, and so forth—not to mention the emergence of the "Christian Right" as a potent political force—demonstrate the continuing importance of Christian points of view, even in the face of manifest pluralism.

The difficulty with that persistent Christian inclination is manifested in many, often very subtle ways. For example, laws mandating a "moment of silence" in schools may seem like a nicely neutral compromise to get around the problems associated with school prayer. But such laws implicitly stigmatize students whose prayer traditions do not typically include silent meditation. Muslims, for example, are more apt to carry out ritual prayer (*salat*) by standing, bowing, and prostrating themselves, none of which they would feel socially comfortable doing during a designated "moment of silence" when most of their peers are sitting quietly with their heads bowed.

Some people advocate turning our attention away from matters that inevitably lead to denominational miscommunication (e.g., public prayer, the public display of religious symbols) and directing them instead to general concerns about morality ("family values") that adherents to all religions (or even those not formally religious at all) can agree on. But one hardly needs to be a theologian to realize that along with different doctrinal beliefs and ritual practices, different religions will have different traditions about what does and does not constitute moral behavior. And even if "the family" is the universal bedrock of the social organization, it does not always have the same structure or espouse the same values. The strongly authoritarian, patriarchal extended families of some traditional societies stand in sharp contrast to the American norm of the somewhat egalitarian, cooperative nuclear family. While the former has a tendency to give way to the latter the longer an immigrant group is in the United States, such an evolutionary process cannot be expected to happen overnight, and in the meantime there are many possible opportunities for miscommunication.

As our exploration into the culture concept has demonstrated, we cannot assume that ours is the only logical or meaningful way to look at the world. In former times, it was possible to ignore this principle, since people, isolated by limited communication and transportation options, rarely encountered those of different background. In a pluralistic society, however, we cannot avoid the necessity to continually weigh our historical traditions (which seem to favor one denomination over all others) against the positive influences of learning to create a society that recognizes and incorporates cultural diversity into its public life.

Discussion

In order to review your familiarity with the issues raised in this chapter, I ask that you do a bit of individual research which would then be very appropriate to share with the other members of your discussion group.

Select any one public policy issue about which religious groups have taken positions in your own particular community (e.g., abortion, the death penalty, immigration reform, school prayer, school vouchers, welfare reform) and review the local history of that controversy. Who are the major "stakeholders" in the controversy (i.e., which individuals or groups are most concerned with the outcome of the debate?)? What incidents or events precipitated the public controversy? Have there been legislative or judicial actions that bear on the outcome of the controversy? What efforts have been made to resolve the conflict? In general, how does the local situation compare/contrast with discussions or actions pertinent to this issue in the nation as a whole? How would you characterize the style of decision making that has prevailed locally during this debate? Would you change it? Why? How? Finally, and most importantly, what are the main dimensions of American *culture* that are at stake in this controversy?

5

SPECIAL CHALLENGES FOR RELIGION
IN A PLURALISTIC SOCIETY

Challenges and Gifts

Participants in the workshops on which this book is based have sometimes expressed frustration, as people of faith who must deal with the myriad complexities of the pluralistic and diverse society described in the preceding chapters. I
have heard and read comments to the effect that learning about cultural diversity represents a surrender to the secular values of the current political order,
which is seen as a barrier to living out one's religious commitments. My response
is reflected in the subtitle of the book: Cultural diversity is a gift, as well as a challenge to contemporary Christians. I believe it is a gift because it calls us to study
and reflect on our assumptions and values, which I take to be the first duty of a
person of faith. I have noted on several occasions and in different ways that I am
not trying to force every user of this book to reach the same conclusions and to
adopt an absolutely relativistic stance by which every manifestation of diversity
is judged to be equally valid in all circumstances. On the contrary, my point is
that in engaging in the guided discussions in this workbook, local groups can
come to a better understanding of their own situations. My only expectation is
that religious professionals will use objective and up-to-date insights from the social sciences when they factor culture into their reflections about issues that arise
in their own communities. The final decision is theirs, and I am well aware of
the fact that certain aspects of the cultural diversity of the United States (sexual

orientation perhaps most obvious among them) simply cannot be accommodated within certain faith traditions. But a response based on freely shared discussion of all available perspectives is always to be desired, even if it ends up confirming foundational principles. As David Cook has noted:

> To say "yes" to one ideology or religion is to reject the alternatives. The problem is that we still have to live and work with people who do not share our beliefs and whose view of the world and reality may be very different. Coping with pluralism will mean understanding other people's points of view and exploring what common ground may be found for joint action. If we refuse to understand what others believe and to respond to the results of such belief as they are expressed in different attitudes and ways of life, we shall retreat to fear, misunderstanding, distrust and even . . . hatred.[1]

That being the case, and in the awareness that the proceeding discussion has emphasized the challenges of cultural diversity, I would like to close this section of the workbook with a brief commentary on the gifts inherent in our current situation. What, in effect, are we positively positioned to accomplish as Christians in a society marked not only by cultural diversity in general but by a structural pluralism in our social and political order?

Trends and Prospects

The great social scientists (e.g., Comte, Marx, Freud) whose ideas dominated the last turn of the century, were convinced that religion had run its course. Although different philosophical reasons stood behind their predictions, they agreed that by the end of the twentieth century, religion would be of purely historical interest. They were wrong, of course. As the sociologist Ronald Johnstone points out in an only slightly exaggerated observation, "In the United States not only does one continue to observe bumper stickers proclaiming Jesus Saves, political candidates mouthing religious clichés, and freshly painted church spires dotting both countryside and town, but one observes amazing new sights and sounds that daily bombard the consciousness."[2] Among those latter manifestations he includes the highly publicized activities of this or that religious cult, the pop cultural fascination with angels, the vigorous sales of Christian rock and pop music, the efforts of the so-called religious right to influence the political discourse, and the elevation of the discussion about the morality of abortion to the status of front-page policy issue. While most of these phenomena have been the work of forces outside the traditional mainstream churches, they do reflect a culture that in spite of its superficial materialism, secularism, and relativism is still (and to a much greater extent than in the other modern industrial democracies) desperately seeking the kinds of service and solace that have always been provided by more formally organized religion.

One very concrete piece of evidence of the enduring vitality of religion and people's commitment to religious values in our society is various measures of the value of new construction of religious facilities, of church/synagogue membership, and of church/synagogue attendance. The value of new religious facilities construction totals in the hundreds of millions of dollars. Even factoring in the different values of 1968 versus 1987 dollars, the level of funding has risen steadily in the past three decades (with a slight dip in the 1970s).[3] Membership in religious organizations declined between 1940 and 1982, but over the course of the past century the figures average out—on the whole there has been "remarkable consistency" in rates of membership.[4] There has been even more consistency with regard to overall rates of attendance, although patterns do vary widely from one denomination to another.[5] Polling data might well be inaccurate, since people have a tendency to overstate their attendance rates. But the fact that they see the need to fudge in the direction of higher attendance indicates where their ideal image of faith commitment is pitched. (A truly secularized society would fudge in the downward direction so as to obscure continued attachment to supposedly outmoded organizational forms.)

Notwithstanding the ambiguities in these measures of continuing religiosity among Americans, it is clear that religion—embodied most visibly in the organized churches even though Americans' "spirituality" is often expressed in more informal settings—continues to serve some enduring and universal functions. First, *religion serves a reinforcement function in society to the degree that it teaches and emphasizes the same norms and values as the society at large.* Religion is one of several institutions (including the family and the educational system) that inculcate such norms and values, and whatever the figures on church attendance may or may not prove, it remains a vitally important one. Each faith tradition certainly teaches its members some norms that are particular to itself, but Christianity taken collectively has certainly been—and continues to be—a major force in underscoring values that are at the core of the American identity. I am not saying that these values (e.g., human dignity and freedom, equality before the law, respect for legitimate authority, faithfulness to one's role) are uniquely Christian. But historically they have become embedded in the American way of looking at the world mainly through organized Christianity. The church is thus gifted in being a recognized and honored vehicle for the transmission of values that form a common ground for most of the disparate elements that make up the patchwork of American cultural diversity.

Religion, in general, and Christianity in America, in particular, have played another role in the process of normative reinforcement to the extent that they have occasionally pushed general norms a bit further than society has initially been willing to embrace. For example, everyone might agree that murder is bad. But the witness of churches (either collectively or individually) against such varied forms of killing as the death penalty, war, abortion, even "ecological racism" (the tendency to dump toxic wastes near communities inhabited by people with the least political and economic clout) has forced a general debate on the ramifications of the basic principle as it is applied in a modern, complex society. There is not necessarily unanimity among the Christian denominations about these issues, and there is certainly no consensus within society that reflects any particular Christian tendency on these matters. But the fact that the moral dimensions of the debate have been articulated through a Christian conscience indicates that just as the churches have a role in reinforcing norms already established and widely accepted, so they have a role in expanding our awareness of the moral dimensions of our political decisions. It is precisely the culturally diverse society that invites Christians to this sort of positive witness, since relatively few other respectable institutions that can serve that function.

A second important function of Christianity in America is its tendency to *bring individuals into meaningful relationships with others in a group*. Churches are among the few institutions in the United States that regularly bring immigrants, social isolates, minorities, and even socially maladjusted people into contact with the "mainstream." They do not, of course, do so consistently or perfectly, but because religious institutions have the reputation for being concerned about people, they do attract relatively large numbers of those in need of meaningful interpersonal contact. As Johnstone notes, "People function better when they feel they have some personal worth and have meaningful, satisfying relationships with other people. To the extent that religious groups provide this service to some who feel isolated [or otherwise excluded], religion is serving the society."[6] Even immigrants who come to this country as adherents to non-Christian religions, and who retain that adherence as a source of internal cohesion for their communities, still are open to some degree of participation in or cooperation with Christian churches, which can be seen as a point of entry into American culture in general. For example, Christmas has become a holiday celebrated by almost all Americans regardless of religious affiliation. As such, its public face often appears to be almost non-Christian (with the focus on materialistic greed and conspicuous consumption). But at the same time, it is also widely recognized as a celebration of "peace on earth, good will to all," sentiments that put the best, most welcoming face on the American scene. Even those who do not physically enter a Christian church for Christmas can be brought into a (temporary, but still powerful) sense of unity through a message promulgated by those churches in the face of diversity and disunity.

Third, religion *helps people face life crises*. Certain experiences (especially death and other kinds of loss) are human universals in that they are occasions for suffering no matter what the specific cultural context might be. Religion is often sought out in such circumstances because it puts such human travails into some sort of eternal perspective, and it provides consolation (if not explicit answers) to what might otherwise be seen as irrational events. The culturally diverse society—which, almost by definition, provides multiple occasions for misunderstanding, hostility, confrontation, and loss—benefits from the presence of an institution that is in a position to offer general solace.

Finally, religion in general and Christianity in particular (because of its strong organizational focus in the United States) *serve as institutions of public welfare*. In older parlance, churches provided the bulk of "charity" for the poor, the sick, orphans, and so forth. The outreach of social services today is more comprehensive, and, while there has been a tendency for government to take over many of these services, there has been countervailing pressure for the private sector to reclaim is prominent place in the effort to meet human material and emotional needs. Different churches place different emphasis on the social service component; some clearly prefer to concentrate on spiritual matters, while others give themselves over in a massive way to community outreach programs. But probably all would agree that ministering to the day-to-day needs of people is a vital component of the more encompassing ministry to their eternal needs. And it is often in the provision of social services that churches of different denominations have successfully worked together—the diverse needs of society at large have prompted something of a recognition of common responsibility on the part of Christians.

Concluding Reflections

The dialogue between religion and culture (or cultures in our diverse society) inevitably leads to changes in both.[7] But we should keep in mind that while some specific forms of religion may undergo change, such trends need not mean that the fundamentals of the faith are compromised or that religion itself disappears into a sea of secularization. The process of religious change appears to be cyclical, rather than linear. If we are concerned about a current slump, we need to put it into a longer historical perspective, and thereby anticipate an eventual rise. And we should remember that the process of cyclical change is a two-way street—religion (even in periods when it superficially seems to be less influential) continues to transform culture just as much as culture transforms the forms and structures of religion. "The phenomenon of religion in one form or another does not disappear," Johnstone concludes. "While it may be in a new form with changes of emphasis . . . it is still what religion always is—namely, an expression of people's ultimate concerns and their basic needs for reassurance about their future—both eternal and in the here and now."[8]

Discussion

1. Visit an art museum whose exhibits cover many centuries of Western art. (If such a museum is not conveniently located for your group, try to locate an illustrated textbook on the history of Western art.) What themes do you find expressed in the explicitly religious art of the past? When do explicitly religious artworks cease to be a prominent feature? Can you discern religious themes in more modern works that are not overtly religious?

2. The percentage of adherents to Islam, Buddhism, and Hinduism is rising rapidly in the United States, despite the persistence of a Christian majority. How do you think these religions will be changed by their contact with a Christian mainstream? What elements of these non-Christian faith traditions might eventually affect mainstream Christianity? (It might make for an interesting discussion if each member of your group selected one of these non-Christian traditions and became the resident "expert" on its beliefs and practices either through reading or interviews with local Muslims, Buddhists, or Hindus.)

3. Convene your group to design a ritual that expresses human relationships with nature. What elements (readings, music, furnishings) would you include? Why? What roles would you assign to the participants? In what ways does your new ritual echo traditional liturgies or other worship services in your faith tradition? In what ways does it represent a departure? How do you account for both the continuities and the points of change?[9]

6

SKILLS FOR EFFECTIVE
INTERCULTURAL COMMUNICATION

Basic Principles

Janice Irvine has written one of the most cogent theoretical analyses of communication across the presumed lines of culture and social group. Although she writes about secular (educational) contexts, her basic position is one with which users of this workbook should feel comfortable. She argues forcefully against "essentialism"—the tendency to reduce cultures to stereotypes, to assume that everyone in an identified group is the same and that their behavioral patterns are fixed and final. She focuses on conversational strategies and communication patterns to demonstrate that culture is a kind of negotiation across very fluid borders rather than a confrontation across immutable barriers. She concludes her discussion with a very useful set of guidelines for effective intercultural communication. I have modified her theoretical discussion of these points and adapted them for the specific contexts that concern us here. The result is the following checklist, which is designed to serve those entering the group discussion phase based on the case studies in the next several chapters.[1]

- *Be prepared to acknowledge and confront our own discomfort and anxieties regarding differences*. Although we should not dwell on the "problems" posed by cultural diversity, neither should we pretend that the situation is an easy one, just in need of a little understanding. If we feel most comfortable with people we think are most like ourselves, that is nothing to be ashamed of—it is a perfectly natural response. But our challenge then is to articulate as best we can what it is about others that makes us uncomfortable. Doing so does not make the differences go away, but it is a necessary first step in a process of meaningful dialogue. Consider the following questions: How do you react when confronted by people you perceive to be different from yourself or what you consider to be the "mainstream"? Do you have strategies to clarify a puzzling situation and to enhance both your own and your community's understanding? Are you able to support and help members of your community understand that communication can and should proceed despite the presumed barriers of cultural difference?

- *Know your own culture first.* Do not assume that your own way of thinking or doing things is somehow "normal," "universal," or "natural." You have culture just like everyone else—culture that was learned, and which can therefore be modified. Engage yourself in an honest appraisal of your own culture: Distinguish the "real" from the "ideal"; separate the core elements (those that really define you and your group in ways that you would be very reluctant to change) from the peripheral ones (those that are essentially things done out of habit that can be modified without doing violence to your fundamental identity). Doing so seems particularly important for those working in ministry—what, after all, do you consider absolutely essential to your faith, as opposed to that which is mainly comfortable habit? The answer will, of course, vary somewhat from one Christian denomination to the next, but all varieties of the Christian tradition can be studied by their members in this way.

- *Get to know the culture of others.* Doing so, as we have seen, means more than simply learning to appreciate a new style of cooking or a different kind of music. It means asking some probing questions about the ways in which people negotiate their personal and group identities across perceived borders.

- *Be aware of power inequities and histories of discrimination.* People who represent what is typically taken to be the "mainstream" should never be in a position of inviting others to assimilate to their standards. A truly culturally diverse Christian community must be one in which all parties change in some ways in order to create a new mainstream that takes all of their positions into account without, of course, compromising the basic tenets of the faith. Doing so is particularly important when dealing with groups that have traditionally been on the short end of the stick and who have ample reason to feel that those who have historically held the power are saying, in effect, "It's our way or the highway."

- *All participants in the cultural diversity dialogue must develop intercultural competence.* It is, of course, vitally important for mainstream people to put aside their stereotypes, prejudices, and historical sense of entitlement and privilege so as to be truly sensitive to the values, aspirations, and ways of thinking and acting that are typical of others. But it is equally important for those others to understand that the mainstream is not an impersonal monolith—they should make an effort to learn mainstream culture, just as mainstream representatives make an effort to learn the culture of "others."

- *Personal commitment is crucial.* It is important for all participants in the dialogue to be willing to take a stand against those individuals or institutions that foster cultural ignorance and perpetuate social inequality. Taking steps to make your church community one that recognizes and honors cultural diversity even as it pursues common faith goals is a kind of prophetic action, and we must always remember that prophets rarely have an easy time of it. Be prepared to face questions, criticisms, even hostility from those in your community who do not yet see the value of what you are attempting to accomplish. Be prepared to defend your own values in favor of diversity in a Christian context.

Theological Reflection

Looking at situations of cultural diversity in Christian perspective involves a process of analysis sometimes referred to as theological reflection (TR), which is basically a method of discernment designed to bring several overlapping perspectives to bear on a group's deliberation of a given issue. There are many published models of TR, and your discussion group can choose any that seems to fit your own style and background. One relatively simple method of TR that has worked well for participants in the workshops on which this book is based is the "tripolar model," which uses three data sources, each of which reveals the presence of God, but in ways that complement rather than duplicate one another. The goal is to attain a balanced view that leads to an informed pastoral action. The three sources are (1) sacred scripture in general and the historical traditions specific to your own denomination or community; (2) the empirical sciences; and (3) your own experience as an aware citizen of the world. Neglect of sacred scripture and allied traditions can result in a decision that is fallibly human. Inattention to the empirical scientific material can result in a decision that separates your faith community from larger patterns that would help put your local issues into a larger perspective. And dismissal of your own experience can result in a conclusion that, while academically sound, misses the dynamic of how people actually live their lives and may thus seem irrelevant and esoteric.

The tripolar model allows participants first to seek out the information that is available in the three sources, then to engage the information in a process of mutual clarification and challenge so as to expand and deepen religious insight, and finally to move from insight through decision to concrete pastoral action. These three steps are sometimes referred to as seeing, judging, and acting.

Kinast has very usefully broken the tripolar model into a four-step process.[2] It begins with the individual (or, preferably, the group) applying a theological reflection to a given issue describing the experience in as much detail as possible. With regard to the following case studies, for example, describe in your own words *what* happened; *who* was involved; *where* the action took place; *when* it took place; *how* the problem/issue came about. Second, it is necessary to "enter the experience." While describing an experience is a necessary prerequisite to further reflection, participants can only truly learn from the experience if they make it their own. To do so, the discussants need to revisit elements of it already described in objective terms, but this time they should (1) treat the "who" as "players," stressing the interactions that link the people together rather than simply identifying them by name and position; (2) deal with the "what" and "when" as if it were a dramatic "plot," setting out the issues or values at stake— in essence, dealing with the question of why there is a conflict in need of some discussion and resolution; and (3) consider the "where" not just in terms of physical space but (especially pertinent for the matters under consideration in this book) in terms of *cultural* space, asking how images, objects, gestures, symbols are used to express a learned, shared, integrated view of life, particularly if different life views are part of the dramatic plot.

The third feature of Kinast's model leads us to learn from the experience. We do so first by seeing how what we've learned from our discussion can serve as an *illustration* of some general principle, which should be one that we have learned via our study of the sacred scripture, empirical literature, and individual and group experience. A case study, even a brief one, probably can be used to illustrate more than one principle, but for the purposes of discussion it may be a good idea to begin with and focus on one that seems to be most clearly in play. Second, we need to find an *application* of that principle, preferably to some analogous situation in our own professional lives. And then we can derive an *interpretation* of that case study by making recommendations for actions that might alleviate the situation in the community under study, as well as in other cases that you have deemed to be analogous.

Although theological reflection on case studies in the abstract can be useful in academic contexts, religious professionals actively engaged in ministry or pastoral work need to be able to carry out the things they have learned in the reflection process in their own work situations. Kinast refers to this, the fourth step of his process, as "enacting the experience." It begins at the personal level; one should leave the reflection session asking how the things that have been learned might affect one's own identity, self-image, motivation, and feelings about oneself. With that degree of self-awareness, the participant can then consider his or her religious professional activities. Several key questions must be addressed: Will this learning experience affect *what* one does? if so, how? if not, why not? Will it affect how one acquires and uses skills in working with individuals, groups, communities, society at large?

Like any effective, dynamic process, this model of TR feeds back on itself in that it not only uses concepts and methods learned from prior study of or experience with theology, but also contributes to the sum of theological insight. It does so because, as Kinast points out, theology can be said to have three aspects. First, and perhaps most obviously, it is the "Word-from-God," and in that sense is, in its essence, transcendent, universal, and authoritative. Yet, as we have seen in this discussion, it is always and necessarily communicated through the limitations of our human nature, which includes our being enmeshed in that "complex whole" we've called culture. Our challenge becomes separating out the essential Word-from-God from the cultural matrix in which it has been historically embedded. Second, theology is the "Word-about-God," which Kinast defines as our faith response to what we believe the Word-from-God really is. Once again, as we have seen, we cannot respond except through the media of our culture—the language, styles of learning, traditions of ritual and storytelling, and so forth. We are not abstract "creatures," but creatures who live in and whose experiences are shaped by the specific cultures in which we interact; as such, there is no way that our faith can be expressed except through the images, gestures, symbols that our culture has provided us with. Of course, as we have seen, it is possible to unlearn or relearn these cultural elements so as to broaden the horizons of our faith response; but we cannot even begin to do so unless we recognize them for what they are—they are the medium of communication, not the ultimate message thereof. And finally, theology is the "Word-to-God," which is how our faith commitment leads us to live our lives. And once again we must recognize that we cannot live except in the context of culture. Saying so does not mean that we have to accept the constraints of our culture without question; but we cannot undo or even modify them to allow us a better way to live out our commitment unless we begin with a clear awareness of what is entailed in living within a culture.

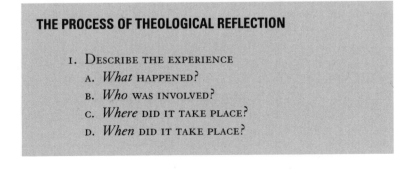

THE PROCESS OF THEOLOGICAL REFLECTION

I. DESCRIBE THE EXPERIENCE
   A. *What* HAPPENED?
   B. *Who* WAS INVOLVED?
   C. *Where* DID IT TAKE PLACE?
   D. *When* DID IT TAKE PLACE?

2. ENTER THE EXPERIENCE
   A. *Players* (INTERACTIONS)
   B. *Plot* (ISSUES OR VALUES AT STAKE)
   C. *Place*
      I.) PHYSICAL SETTING
      II.) CULTURAL FACTORS (SEEN IN USE OF IMAGES, OBJECTS, GESTURES, SYMBOLS, AND SO FORTH)
      • INTEGRATION
      • LEARNING
      • SHARING
3. LEARN FROM THE EXPERIENCE
   A. THE EXPERIENCE AS *illustration*
   B. THE EXPERIENCE AS *application*
   C. THE EXPERIENCE THROUGH *interpretation*
4. ENACTING THE EXPERIENCE
   A. PERSONAL
      I.) IDENTITY
      II.) SELF-IMAGE
      III.) MOTIVATION
      IV.) FEELINGS ABOUT ONESELF
   B. MINISTERIAL
      I.) WHAT ONE DOES
      II.) HOW ONE MINISTERS
      III.) SKILLS ONE DEVELOPS IN WORKING WITH
      • INDIVIDUALS
      • GROUPS
      • COMMUNITIES
      • SOCIETY AT LARGE
   C. THEOLOGICAL
      I.) THE WORD-FROM-GOD (COMMUNICATED THROUGH NATURE AND CULTURE)
      II.) THE WORD-ABOUT-GOD (FAITH AS MEDITATED BY CULTURE)
      III.) THE WORD-TO-GOD (LIVING THE CHRISTIAN LIFE IN THE CONTEXT OF ONE'S CULTURE)

The Acquisition of Cultural Competence

Making a religious community (parish or other) one that incorporates a culturally diverse perspective into its life is never easy, because it means crossing into other people's cultural space and having them bring their customs and values into "my space." It is perhaps easier to do so when dealing with those of clearly different racial or ethnic groups, since the diversity is so obvious that it can hardly be ignored. But as we have suggested in this workbook, the nature of diversity is much more subtle, extending even into areas of "our own space" that are more widely differentiated than we might feel comfortable admitting. When we commit ourselves to a project of deepening our understanding of and appreciation for cultural diversity, we are at the same time committing ourselves to becoming cross-culturally "competent"—putting ourselves, as it were, in the cultural "space" of people who might not think or behave as we do.

Religious professionals, unlike others who are concerned with the acquisition of cultural competence, can usually assume that there is some commonality resulting from adherence to a shared set of faith principles. But common faith must not be mistaken for a common set of values when it comes to the ways in which we live out our faith commitments. For example, we can identify several principles (among many others, to be sure) that seem to characterize the way mainstream Americans structure their lives:

- Personal control
- Predisposition in favor of change and variety
- Competition
- Individualism
- Future orientation
- Directness of expression
- Informality
- Precision about time
- Focus on the duration of life
- Emphasis on the nuclear family

By contrast, other cultures might emphasize the following:

- Fate, destiny, "God's will"
- Predisposition in favor of tradition
- Cooperation
- Group orientation
- Past orientation

- Indirectness of expression
- Formality
- Precision about human interaction (e.g., ways of showing respect)
- Focus on the quality of life
- Emphasis on the extended family

Cultural competence refers to a set of skills that allow individuals to increase their understanding and appreciation of the patterns of values such as the preceding—the cultural differences and similarities within, among, and between groups. Achieving cultural competence requires a willingness and ability to draw on community-based values, traditions, and customs and to work with knowledgeable persons of and from the community so as to develop targeted interventions, communications, and other support mechanisms. Cultural competence involves a continuum of attitudes and behaviors:

- Understanding one's own cultural background
- Acknowledging that other members of the community might have different cultures, values systems, beliefs, and behaviors
- Recognizing that cultural difference is not synonymous with cultural inferiority
- Learning about the cultures of other members of the community
- Adapting programs to take cultural diversity into respectful account

Activities and programs of a culturally diverse community can become means to cultural competence to the extent that they

- demonstrate sensitivity to and understanding of cultural differences in program design, implementation, and evaluation
- acknowledge culture as a predominant force in shaping behaviors, values, and institutions
- acknowledge and accept that cultural differences exist and have an impact on the way people work in groups, teams, communities, and so forth
- believe that diversity within cultures is as important as diversity among cultures
- respect the special, culturally defined needs of various components of their target populations
- recognize that concepts such as "family" and "community" have different nuances of meaning in various culturally defined groups—even groups within the same overall culture
- recognize that taking the best of both worlds enhances the capacity of all.

Since the suggested format for using this workbook is in a discussion group, it is very important that the group itself model that which it hopes to inspire— a workable, culturally diverse setting that honors and respects the various aspects of difference even as it helps participants work toward common goals. Remember that developing such cultural competence is an ongoing process—it is not a one-time acquisition.

The process begins with the logistics of the group meeting itself. Some pointers that might be helpful in the planning of such meetings are as follows:

- *Select dates and times for meetings that do not conflict with cultural or religious holidays and events.*
- *Select meeting facilities that are accessible.* Note that accessibility may include, but is not limited to, the use of personal assistants, special dietary requirements or preferences (if refreshments are to be served), sign-language interpretation services or listening devices, large-print or Braille materials, transportation assistance, child or other dependent care, ramps or other accommodations for wheelchairs.
- *Determine the extent to which participants will require the use of a cultural broker or interpreter in order to participate fully in the meeting.* It is extremely important that these discussion meetings not be seen as "us" making plans that affect "them." "They" must be included in the discussions, and steps must be taken to facilitate their inclusion.

In the meeting itself, it is important to be conscious of several ways in which communication can be enhanced or impeded. (This is a delicate balancing act: It is unwise to become so conscious of communication as it is going on that no communication is possible.) Pay particular attention to the *nonverbal* aspects of communication since the most important messages of communication across presumed cultural borders are often conveyed in such hidden devices. For example:

- *Silence.* Mainstream Americans are often uncomfortable with silence and fear that a discussion is bogging down if there is not constant verbalization. But silence may also represent serious reflection or respect and should not be filled in just for the sake of presumed "content."
- *Distance.* Preferred distance from one participant to another in a discussion and the arrangement of the furnishings of a room to facilitate discussion vary from group to group. Round tables seem to work better in most cases than chairs arranged in a lecture/classroom format, but keep in mind that in some cultures it is uncomfortable to maintain eye contact (which, by contrast, is so very important to mainstream Americans) so that a round table might impede discussion.

- *Facial expression, gestures, body language.* Some cultures are very free with such expressions (and, in the stereotype at least, women in general are more so than men) while others cultivate a greater reserve. Keep in mind that extravagant gestures or expansive body language may not indicate unusual enthusiasm—they may simply be conventional ways of making a point—just as an impassive face or controlled body language may not indicate coldness or indifference.

The point of acquiring and developing the skills of cultural competence, like any rules of etiquette, is to make the maximum number of people feel comfortable in social settings in which they commonly participate. Learning occurs in many different ways in many different settings. Each individual places value on and has preferences for how he or she receives, processes, and uses information—ways that are almost certainly shaped by the diverse cultural factors discussed previously. This workbook was not designed so that religious professionals could talk *about* issues of cultural diversity in the abstract; it was meant to nurture the skills of cultural competence so that diverse groups of people, aware of their own cultures and the cultures of others, could engage in meaningful discussions whenever issues of cultural diversity do arise.

Applying the Discussion Format

The case studies that follow provide the context in which such discussions can take place. While the cases can certainly provide material for individual reflection, they are most effective when used in group settings. It is recommended that when a group is convened to engage in such discussions, each member familiarize him- or herself with the basic principles of cultural diversity as previously presented and also engage in the self-examination suggested in the questions attached to the earlier chapters. The format and layout of the group meetings should take into account the principles set out in the previous section. The discussion itself should adhere as far as possible to the style of theological reflection presented earlier.

Keep in mind that there are no right or wrong solutions to any of the case studies. The point is to apply what participants have learned about the principles of cultural diversity, first to probe the situation presented in the cases, and then (and most importantly) to analogous situations in the real professional experiences of the participants. I might even go so far as to suggest that establishing a discussion process that is sensitive to, and that tries to live up to, the ideal of culturally competent reflection on diversity is almost more important than any specific conclusions that are reached as a result of that discussion. Those conclusions may well change as circumstances change, but the format and the process, which reflect a set of values and attitudes and behaviors, can be an enduring legacy in the community served by religious professionals who participate.

Keep in mind a caution noted in an earlier chapter: The point of these exercises is not to force every religious congregation or community into a particular model of cultural diversity. It is important that each group come to a decision about what is feasible and desirable as well as in harmony with the teachings of its particular faith tradition. But it is important that such decisions be informed about the content and process of cultural diversity so that decisions do not reflect mere "conventional wisdom." There is no single "right" answer to any of the questions attached to the following case studies—only the answer that is "right" for your particular group. But I hope that learning more about what cultural diversity involves, and developing some skills in the process of acquiring cultural competence will make for a more fruitful discussion in support of your group's decision.

7

A CASE STUDY IN
COMMUNICATION ACROSS ETHNIC BORDERS

The Case Study

Riverdale Community Church is located in a middle-to-upper income suburban area. It is known for having the largest and most successful adult religious education program in the area. In the past five years, people from Southeast Asia and Korea have become an increasingly visible presence in the congregation and have been very eager to take part in the educational programs of the church. Mr. John Kim, who is of Korean descent, is a member of the church's board of trustees. He told the pastor, Rev. Ted Jones, that newly arrived Asians are enthusiastic about education, but very reluctant to join the program as it is currently constituted. He pointed out that most of the classes are led by lay members of the congregation and that religious insights are usually taught by having participants do some fairly intimate sharing about how Scripture relates to their own lives. But the culture from which they come prohibits such intimacy in groups of mixed gender outside the family circle, and so they would feel uncomfortable in the classes even if their English were better. They would much prefer to have a separate but equal program of religious instruction delivered in lecture format by a recognized authority figure in the church, such as one of the ordained ministers.

Leah Watson, the director of religious education, objects to Mr. Kim's request, noting that while sensitivity to ethnic diversity is a fine thing, the church cannot afford either financially or in terms of group unity to sponsor separate programs for every conceivable constituency. If a concession were made for one group, then there would be no end to the groups that would want to opt out, and soon the church would have numerous small congregations instead of one united in faith. Ms. Watson told Rev. Jones, "If people of Asian heritage really want to be part of this church, then they should adapt themselves to our way of doing things and not expect to have their own traditions take precedence."

Rev. Jones is inclined to be sympathetic to cultural differences, but he is also sensitive to Ms. Watson's concern about appearing to disvalue the integrity of the congregation. He wonders if perhaps Mr. Kim and his friends will agree to participate if he asks one of the Asians to design some new banners for the entryway and allows one of the Scripture passages to be read in Korean or Vietnamese at Sunday services.

Discussion and Analysis

This case study represents the sort of situation most people think of first when they consider the problem of the culturally diverse church. It features a middle-class congregation (most probably with a majority of "Anglos") trying to welcome a newer immigrant stream but finding that certain values and practices that they take for granted are misunderstood by the newcomers. There seems to be a danger that the positions of the various interest groups will harden into adversarial stances on the assumption that the cultural divide is just too wide to be bridged without doing violence to either set of traditions.

How might a perspective on culture informed by social science assist the Riverdale Church in dealing with this perceived problem?

Let us return to one of our basic principles of culture: It is *learned* behavior, which means that it is not set in stone. There may be a tendency to ignore this fact in this case because by convention we think of Asians as not only members of a different ethnic group, but as members of a different race. In the common view, "racial" characteristics are inborn and hence not amenable to change. But what is at issue here is not the Asians' "racial" characteristics, but the customs that constitute their repertoire of things they have learned about behaving in religious settings. As such, the fact that the newcomers' traditional culture gives them certain expectations about social interactions is not to be dismissed; but it does not mean that they are incapable of learning new patterns of interaction. Indeed, one can only assume that, having lived in the United States for a while, they have already adopted some new behaviors as a result of going to school or getting a job. Given the relatively affluent nature of the neighborhood served by the Riverdale Church, it is likely that the newcomers are working in skilled or professional positions; it is not likely that they are living in a stereotypical Chinatown where their ancestral culture could be preserved without much modification.

But it is just as important to keep in mind another principle discussed earlier: "We" have culture, too, in the sense that we live in accordance with open-ended, flexible patterns of learned behavior. Adult education programs must certainly be operated in conformity with certain guidelines and norms, lest they collapse into disorganized jumbles. But organization need not mean inflexibility. The church's preference for certain procedures is a matter of cultural habituation (behavior that the church's leaders have learned and grown comfortable with), not the result of hard-and-fast rules.

In sum: Yes, there is a gap of cultural communication, but no, it is not one that reflects inborn traits that neither side cannot modify.

But there are other considerations to be taken into account. For example, Leah Watson and Rev. Jones seem to assume that Mr. Kim is the unchallenged spokesman for all the Asians. As noted earlier, sometimes the person who comes forward to speak for his community has an agenda of his own. He *might* be conveying a widely shared viewpoint, but then again, he might not. In this case, Mr. Kim is of Korean heritage. Can we automatically assume that even if he speaks for all the other Koreans (itself a proposition we would need to test further and not simply take for granted), he also speaks for the Vietnamese? Moreover, are the norms he speaks of (regarding speaking of personal matters in a mixed group, or preferring to learn from recognized experts or authorities) really shared by all Koreans—let alone by all Asians? Maybe they are, but we would certainly want to investigate beyond simply taking his word for it. And is the real problem here talking in a mixed-gender group, or is it doing so in front of Anglos?

Remember, too, that culture has both "ideal" and "real" facets. Perhaps all that Mr. Kim says is true—but if so, it is probably only true of the "ideal" culture. The people he speaks for may well have already learned to separate things they must do in order to survive in a new cultural context from the things they learned were appropriate in ancestral times. Forcing people to choose the "real" over the "ideal" is seldom a good idea; but it is certainly a good idea to keep in mind when working in culturally diverse settings that people often make the choice of their own accord, using their own means.

Remember that culture is shared; but it is important to find out how widely a certain trait is shared before we assume that it constitutes a true pattern. Moreover, we want to find out how intensely it is held among those who share it. Is the disinclination to participate in the group format something that represents the deepest bedrock elements of the culture—something that, if tampered with, would destroy the community—or is it something that the Asians themselves are already in the process of changing in light of other experiences they are having in school or at work? In other words, to what extent is it integrated into a larger pattern, such that change would unravel relationships beyond those at the church?

Rev. Jones's solution is an example of a proposal that is praiseworthy in and of itself, but that probably misses the mark with regard to the problem at hand. He has made an error common to those who misunderstand "culture" as restricted mainly to external symbols. Banners can be an important way to set the tone for those entering the church, and probably most people would welcome adding an "Asian accent" to their expression. Having readings done in other languages (probably in addition to, rather than instead of, English) would be a bit cumbersome, but again not particularly threatening to anyone. But culture is really about how people interrelate and interact; all the banners in the world will not make much of a difference if the Asians are still uncomfortable in social situations that include non-Asians because of subtle nuances of interactive style that have little to do with how the church is decorated.

In our discussion of ethnicity, we pointed out that in many cases, the maintenance of ethnic boundaries is more important than the specific content of the presumed ethnic cultures. Immigrant groups, in particular, may find it useful to maintain their ethnic identity even as—indeed, particularly when—they adopt the ways of the place to which they have immigrated. Their identity serves as a sort of reassuring anchor in the midst of a process of rapid and stressful change. The host community may be puzzled at the apparently irrational desire on the part of their newcomers to maintain their separateness even when, to the outsider, it looks as if they are already assimilating to mainstream culture. Although there may be apparent movement in the direction of a unified set of behavioral and attitudinal norms, the host culture should be sensitive to the value of helping the newcomers maintain the perceived boundary—as long as that boundary does not harden into a wall that blocks out further communication.

We must also consider the special role of language in this process of boundary maintenance. It is probably true, given the nature of the Riverdale community, that the Asians can get by in English quite well. But language is more than simply a neutral means of conveying information. Language is the vehicle of culture. Even if the Asians can convey certain obvious things (such as the content of a passage from Scripture) in English without much difficulty, there are always certain matters that defy translation, even by fluently bilingual people— for example, nuances of expression that connote respect and honor, which are typically very important in Asian cultures, are drained of cultural meaning when they are translated literally into English. Conversely, the American preference for calling people by their first names is an expression of the important value Americans place on equality in a democracy—we tend to believe that we are showing respect to people when we treat them as equals. But in other cultures, declining to use an honorific title would not indicate respect, but the exact opposite.

This latter point might lead us to conclude that true and complete translation is never really possible ("to translate is to betray" as an old proverb has it), so that distinct cultural groups can never fully communicate. In the technical sense, this may be so, but it is a poor recipe for achieving a workable culturally diverse setting. Creating "separate but equal" facilities is usually not a workable option from the budgetary standpoint, even if it sounds as if it might be the solution most respectful of cultural diversity. The number of distinctive groups is potentially infinite, and it is simply impractical to treat each of them differently. No church could possibly muster the resources to provide separate but equal services to every conceivable cultural group within its borders. And even if it were possible to do so, it would certainly violate the principle of a church as a people united in faith.

How, then, can we respect cultural difference without hardening those differences into unscalable walls?

Questions for Group Discussion

Note: The following, and the questions associated with all the other case study chapters, are structured for group discussion, although they can certainly be used as guides for individual reflection as well.

1. Who are the key players in this case study? What values or attitudes do you think account for their actions? To what extent are those values and attitudes the products of culture (as opposed to those that are individual/psychological)?
2. What features of the social setting do you think are most important in understanding the issues at Riverdale? (Keep in mind that the social setting can be interpreted on several levels: the church itself; the city or region in which the church is located; the United States as a whole).
3. How do you assess the interplay of "racial" and "ethnic" stereotypes in this case, and how might those stereotypes be most effectively overcome?
4. Which cultural factors do you think are most important to take into consideration in making a pastoral decision on behalf of the Riverdale community? (You may choose from those discussed in this chapter, from those discussed elsewhere in this workbook, or from other sources that your own experience may have suggested to you.)
5. Based on your analysis, what plan of action can your group suggest to the Riverdale Church? (If you prefer, your plan might be couched in terms of

several possible options, rather than a single recommendation. In either case, make sure that your plan is one that can be generally acknowledged by all members of your discussion group.)

6. What lessons have you learned from your analysis of the Riverdale situation that you could apply to your own congregation or community? Try to come up with a case study describing an analogous situation in your own setting and discuss the specific cultural factors that figure in your analysis of your own community. To what extent are they the same factors that seemed to be important in your analysis of Riverdale? In what ways are they different? Would you come up with the same plan for your own community as you did for Riverdale? If so, why? If not, why not?

8

A CASE STUDY IN RELIGIOUS PLURALISM

The Case Study

Rev. Fred Samuels is an ordained Presbyterian minister, but at Bigtime State University (BSU), he serves as chaplain for a consortium of campus religious foundations, including those serving Methodist, Lutheran, and Church of Christ communities. He is the current coordinator of the campus ministry board, which also includes Father James Grant, Father Edmond Freeman, and Rabbi David Hoff, respectively the Episcopalian, Roman Catholic, and Jewish chaplains. The board has decided to contribute to BSU's annual Cultural Diversity Recognition Week with a series of lectures and concerts, and an ecumenical prayer service. The members reasoned that in a highly secularized institution such as BSU, it was important for those representing religious interests to set aside denominational distinctions and celebrate their different but equally important responses to the negative aspects of secular materialism.

Rev. Samuels was surprised, however, when he was approached by Professor Martha Gregory, a member of the Department of Philosophy who serves as faculty advisor to the Wiccan community on campus. Professor Gregory said that the members of her group were interested in participating in the board's program and added that, given the ministers' stated interest in diversity, they should welcome the addition of this increasingly important element in the religious mix of the campus.

Rev. Samuels told Professor Gregory that he would have to consult with the other members of the board, who turned out not to be enthusiastic. Father Grant pointed out that their group represented a Christian orientation and that if non-Christian groups wanted to be part of the program, they could do so under their own auspices. Rabbi Hoff pointedly added, "Well, I assumed that our board represented a Judeo-Christian tradition, not just a Christian one." Father Freeman said that of course that was so, but the real issue was not that the Wiccans weren't part of the Judeo-Christian tradition, but that they were not, by university charter, official members of the ministry board. But Rev. Samuels pointed out that neither were the campus Muslims, Buddhists, or Hindus, although they were all being included in the ecumenical prayer service. Father Grant said that as long as it was important to include everyone, then what about the small, but vocal group of Native Americans who had started their own shamanic healing services?

The board finally decided that while in principle it would be a good idea to include every possible religious group on campus—they were, after all, celebrating diversity—doing so would make a shambles of the program. It would simply get too big and unwieldy. Instead of demonstrating to the campus at large the importance of religious values in the modern world, the program would only demonstrate the ineptitude of the religious representatives on campus. Informed of their decision, Professor Gregory sadly concluded that the ministers were really only concerned because Wicca is considered an "alternative" religion that many ill-informed people still associate with Satanism. In an editorial, the campus newspaper endorsed her conclusions and charged the ministry board with discriminating against the Wiccans. The board's tolerance for religious pluralism, the editorial stated, extended only as far as the boundaries of traditional, formal religious organizations.

Discussion and Analysis

This case is superficially similar to the one discussed in chapter 7. Many of the comments regarding the pros and cons of recognizing a great number of different groups still hold true. But there are some special issues involved in this particular case that call for additional discussion.

In the first place, the context this time is not a once-homogeneous church gradually making way for ethnically diverse newcomers. It is, rather, a university campus—a secular community whose interest in cultural diversity probably results in some additional political and social constraints on the religious representatives, who must function as part of a much larger society lacking in the decision-making autonomy of a church congregation. The Riverdale Church discussed in chapter 7 could come up with a solution to its problem based on the needs and values of its own members, with due attention paid to the specific doctrinal, liturgical, or operational guidelines by which the church operated. But at BSU, the context for the ministers' decision making is not only one of ethnic diversity but also of religious pluralism. The members of the board undoubtedly share some basic values, but they cannot really rely on being able to marshal their followers' energies on the basis of common faith.

At the Riverdale Church, we could presume that the Asians were coming to the church of their own accord and had some predisposition to accommodate to the congregation's norms, even if they were not entirely comfortable doing so. But at BSU, the diversity initiative is part of a program of outreach (or, more cynically, of public relations); it is a way of "selling" the religious perspective to a community that has no particular commitment to that point of view. The interests of the various groups represented by the ministry board at BSU must surely be weighed against the pressures they face as people trying to practice their respective faiths in the midst of a highly secularized social atmosphere. At Riverdale, we could assume that all the parties to the discussion shared a commitment to the basic tenets of Christianity. At BSU, there is a wider "audience" of people who have no such commitment. What might be divisive within a church that prefers to think of itself as a faith community might or might not be politically adaptive on campus. Moreover, the specific activity in which the cultural diversity issue plays out at BSU is a one-time celebration for the benefit of a more or less transient population, as opposed to an ongoing program of a permanent church congregation.

Questions for Group Discussion

1. The preceding analysis suggests that the differences in the social settings of BSU and Riverdale might result in different resolutions to a roughly similar problem. Which specifically *cultural* issues would you want to explore further in order to reach a pastoral decision particular to the BSU situation?

2. The members of the BSU ministry board seem to be ignoring (up to a point) their own pluralism in favor of presenting a united "religious" front against secular values. What are the advantages and disadvantages of downplaying their internal differences?

3. The "point" up to which they ignore their differences is the participation of the Wiccans. What do you make of their various rational explanations for excluding the Wiccans? If there is covert discrimination against the latter, as Professor Gregory and the editorialist charge, do you think it is

at all justified in this context? How would Rev. Samuels and his colleagues go about learning more about Wicca? Do you think it is worthwhile for them to do so?

4. What do *you* think is the most important thing that the board should want to accomplish by participating in the campus-wide program? How might that goal best be reached? (You may, if you wish, suggest several viable options rather than a single recommendation, but try to find a solution that all members of your group can live with.)

5. There are other contexts in which people in ministry might work that are like a college campus in terms of being primarily secular institutions with a pluralistic population—for example, chaplaincy programs in hospitals, prisons, the military, or at airports. What lessons learned from the BSU case might be commonly applied in these analogous situations? What are some of the specific factors involved in those other contexts that would make their particular challenges of pluralism different from those at BSU? Carefully discuss the interplay of race, ethnicity, social class, gender, sexual orientation, age, and condition of disability in each of these pluralistic settings; in what ways are these configurations similar from one context to another? in what ways do they differ?

6. What lessons have you learned from your analysis of the BSU situation that could apply to a situation in a community that you know of or work in? Try to come up with a case study describing an analogous situation in your own setting and discuss the specific cultural factors that figure in your analysis of your own community. To what extent are they the same factors that seem to be important at BSU? In what ways are they different? Would you come up with the same recommendation(s) for your own community as you did for BSU? If so, why? If not, why not?

9

A CASE STUDY IN SOCIAL
CLASS AND SOCIAL RESPONSIBILITY

The Case Study

St. Perpetua Roman Catholic Church is located in a once rural area that has in the past few years become the most trendy, upscale neighborhood of a rapidly growing Sunbelt city. It now has the reputation as the "yuppie parish," much to the chagrin of the remaining farm families who have been parishioners for decades. Aaron Bell, one of the farmers, has expressed his concerns to the pastor, Father Louis Mills. Mr. Bell feels that the newcomers have completely taken over the parish council and all the social activities of the parish community. He admits that since they are now in the majority it is only right for them to have the biggest say, but he thinks Father Mills ought to do more to encourage them to take the old families more into account.

The last straw, as far as Mr. Bell was concerned, was when Lance Gorsebush, the wealthy owner of a chain of fashionable bagel boutiques, donated a large sum of money to the parish. Father Mills, with the support of the parish council, decided to use the money to build a new rectory, overriding the votes of Mr. Bell and his allies, who were hoping to establish a food bank for migrant farmworkers. To make matters worse in Mr. Bell's eyes, the rectory was being designed by the city's hottest architectural firm, and the plans called for the construction of an undeniably beautiful, but decidedly lavish building of up-to-the-minute style. There was to be a swimming pool and sauna, a gourmet kitchen, a minigym, and every other amenity one could think of. Mr. Bell was deeply disappointed and told Father Mills that it was a disgrace for a man of the cloth to live in such a palace. Father Mills explained that the decision to build the new rectory was the result of a democratic vote. Moreover, now that St. Perpetua was located in such a fine part of town, it had to blend in. The shabby old rectory was bringing down the tone of the neighborhood.

Father Mills also pointed out that it is important for the church to be an integral part of the culture in which it finds itself, and a house that the parishioners would feel comfortable visiting was one way to make sure that the church would continue to be relevant to their lives. A food bank, while an eminently worthy project in the abstract, was really the responsibility of a parish in a poor district, a parish that shared the culture of poverty with those who would be served by the facility. The people of St. Perpetua would certainly volunteer to go out to work at a food bank downtown from time to time, but they certainly wouldn't want it next door. Putting it there would only make it more difficult for the church to relate to its surroundings. The new rectory, by contrast, would facilitate such a relationship.

Discussion and Analysis

We have noted previously that social class in America is an achieved status that is largely defined by lifestyle choices and tied to the possession and use of material property. The affluent people of the "new" St. Perpetua are clearly used to certain material markers of their position in the community. To the extent that they appear to think of the church as one of their possessions, they want to see it decked out in the same material trappings.

This case challenges us and the values that we as Christians bring to the question of inculturation, the process by which the Gospel is made relevant to non-Western cultures. By analogy, we are likely to oppose the death penalty as long as the people on death row whose stories make the evening news are attractive, articulate, and wrongly accused of their crimes, but we have second thoughts about our principles when it comes to the execution of unpleasant and obviously guilty characters. Here, we find ourselves in general sympathy with the goals of inculturation as long as it is a matter of the church accommodating itself to the marginalized and oppressed whose cause we have, by and large, come to adopt as proper for Christians in our time. It is much harder for us to think about the positive values of inculturation when the setting is a community that is already at the top of the heap and that espouses ideals of competitive materialism that seem out of keeping with Christian values. Can the Gospel become inculturated in such a setting? *Should* it?

The situation in this case study is perhaps overstated for purposes of discussion, but it is not that far from ordinary reality. It is a commonplace observation that in America church affiliation has always been a factor of the class hierarchy. In the traditional South, for example, the elites were Episcopalians, and the lower orders were Baptist, with Presbyterians and Methodists making up the middle class. And even within the same denomination, class differences are not hard to detect. Crumbling old inner-city Catholic parishes stand in stark contrast to gleaming suburban facilities; the basic architecture of the former might be finer, but the latter will usually have state-of-the-art utilities, nice furnishings, lovely landscaping, and ample space for offices, meetings, and classes. It goes without saying that congregations living in poverty cannot be expected to contribute to the upkeep of their parishes in the manner of affluent communities.

In the ideal, we probably think it shocking that churches, of all social institutions, should be caught up in the lifestyle-and-possessions ranking of the rest of American society. But it is doubtful that most of us would support a share-the-wealth program whereby all collections went into a common fund and then were redistributed equally to all churches in a given region, so that all could live within the same budgetary constraints. Such a socialistic approach would appear to violate some other very important American values.

The question remains, however, whether the widespread and taken for granted class hierarchy that marks American religion as an institution of the larger society can or should be addressed by a church committed to inculturation and cultural diversity. Are Mr. Gorsebush and Father Mills correct in asserting that, in effect, it would be just as wrong to force the people of the "new" St. Perpetua to live as if they were poor as it would be to force any parish community to adjust to a culture other than their own?

There are some key points to reflect on in discussing this issue. First, class in America is, as we have said, considered to be *achieved* rather than ascribed status. And in America, the ideal (if not the reality) of class mobility is a critical point in our culture. Second, the principles of American democracy do not necessarily involve a strict "majority rules" approach—there is room (indeed, a real necessity) to achieve compromise when diverse groups live under the same political system. Third, the principle of inculturation is not a matter of the church simply acquiescing to whatever culture it finds; it is a matter of working within the culture in order to call culture to transcend itself in the name of higher values.

Questions for Group Discussion

1. Who are the key players in this case study? What values or attitudes do you think account for their actions? To what extent are those values and attitudes the products of culture (as opposed to those that are individual/psychological)?
2. What features of the social setting (both the local community and the wider American society) do you think are most important in understanding the conflict at St. Perpetua?
3. To what extent do you think that the questions of material possession and lifestyle choice as seen at St. Perpetua reflect a *system* of American class (as opposed to factors particular to this one community)?
4. Which do you think is of greater importance in this case: the principle of helping the poor, or the principle of a church that comes in the trappings of the culture it wishes to serve? Are these two values necessarily in conflict? Can you see any way to reconcile them?
5. Are there any aspects of the culture of competitive materialism typical of the American upper and middle classes that can be incorporated into a dialogue that helps the St. Perpetua community transcend itself—or is that culture itself the very thing that must be transcended? In other words, can community be forged out of the divergence of values and lifestyle choices represented at St. Perpetua?
6. Based on your analysis of this case study, what plan might you come up with to help the people of St. Perpetua? Assume that the rectory versus food bank issue is already a done deal—what steps can be taken to avoid such misunderstandings in the future? Your plan might take the form of several options rather than a single recommendation, although it should be something that all members of your group can stand by.
7. What lessons have you learned from your analysis of the St. Perpetua case that could apply to a situation in your own congregation or community? In what ways does your community differ from St. Perpetua? In what ways are they similar? Which *cultural* factors might need to be considered in coming up with a solution to the specific problems of your own community? Is your plan for your own community different from or similar to the one you recommended for St. Perpetua? Why?

10

A CASE STUDY IN GENDER RIGHTS

The Case Study

Marianne Jamerson holds an MBA from the Harvard Business School, and she founded a highly successful management consulting firm. She is currently in her third term as chair of her city's chamber of commerce. At the moment she is campaigning for a seat on the county commission, an election that polls indicate she will win handily. She has raised three fine children on her own after the death of her husband. She is a longtime member of the Taylor Road United Methodist Church and has always been an enthusiastic volunteer when it came to church projects.

Elroy Watkins, an attorney specializing in real estate law, is also a member of the Taylor Road Church. Ms. Jamerson was shocked to learn that Mr. Watkins had recently been hired by the bishop's office to help them with the sale of some property. She had no qualms about Watkins's qualifications—he was clearly the best person in town to give advice on that particular issue. What bothered her, though, was that he was being paid his regular fee. By contrast, she had been called in by her own bishop, as well as by his colleagues in adjoining regions, to conduct staff training workshops. She believed that she was as much an expert in that area of business as Watkins was in his, and yet she had been expected to do the work for nothing, whereas he had gotten paid. After making some inquiries, she came to see that there was a pattern in such matters: Alice Butterworth, who owned a landscaping firm, was expected to provide services to the church for nothing, while

Maynard Kemp, the electrician, and Paul Milburn, the air conditioner repairman, were always paid for work they did at the church, even though all were members of the congregation. She remembered that the church governing board had requested that a female minister not be assigned to their congregation, despite the fact that the woman in question had graduated from one of the finest seminaries and came with outstanding references from her previous posting in another state. There were several women on the current staff, but they were either teachers, secretaries, or housekeepers. All of the key leadership positions were occupied by men.

Ms. Jamerson was hurt to realize that the church she had loved and had served so faithfully was probably guilty of gender discrimination, and she wondered how she could have been blind to this problem for so long. Some of her friends tell her that if she really feels that strongly about it, she should quit the church—as a public figure now, her departure would certainly bring the problem out into the open. Others, however, tell her that she will be more effective arguing from within; she should use the goodwill she has built up in the church to work to influence it to change. Still others, to be sure, insist that she is making a mountain out of a molehill, because all the cases she mentioned might well be explained by particular circumstances and not in terms of some general, deliberate pattern of discrimination. (Mr. Watkins might have waived his personal fee, but he did not think it would be ethical to ask the members of his staff, who were working with him on the case, to work for his church on a *pro bono* basis; Mr. Kemp's business was known to be failing and it was important to give him financial support; Mr. Milburn might waive his own labor costs, but could not afford to donate all the expensive equipment that he installed; the female minister was newly married and planning to get pregnant soon, which meant that she would not be able to devote her full energies to her new position; all the other staff had been hired on the basis of their talents and prior experience.)

There are even a few acquaintances who tell her flat out that she is misguided. The fact is, they tell her, that men supporting families need to be compensated financially, while women can afford to work as volunteers. And no matter what anyone says, the very idea of a female minister is a violation of all the most cherished traditions of the church. It's one thing, they say, for a woman to rise to prominence in business or politics—the values of the secular world permit such things to happen. But the church need not conform to such values when they conflict with longstanding "family values" as taught by the church.

Discussion and Analysis

Although we might casually label Ms. Jamerson's argument as an objection to "sexism," she is more clearly taking a position with regard to *gender* inequality. It is, after all, a perceived inconsistency in the role behaviors assigned to the sexes to which she is objecting. She is arguing that while our culture at large is hardly innocent of gender discrimination, it has at least moved toward some sort of official recognition that such inequalities should be redressed. An inculturated American church, sensitive to the values of the society at large, should therefore recognize and honor the distinctive role of women while acknowledging that it is wrong to continue to consign them to patterns of behavior that no longer accord with either common practice or legal norms.

Ms. Jamerson is also implicitly making a case about a church's approach to governance and discussion. It is, after all, a typically American trait to want to explore all possible angles of a controversial issue before reaching a decision. But churches, conscious of the need to conform to doctrinal norms (and, in this case, sensitive to the place of the local church within a wider hierarchy), cannot always engage in the sort of open discourse that might be typical of a secular organization. Moreover, while it is likely that all the hiring decisions Ms. Jamerson investigated were made by what seem like openly democratic means, she had to wonder whether the decisionmakers were all literally part of the "old boy network," and therefore how open the discussions were in reality. The church elders were no doubt convinced that their decisions had been made democratically; Ms. Jamerson implicitly raises the issue of whether decisions affecting gender can ever be made democratically by an organization that starts out with a gender bias.

Churches seem to be comfortable with inculturation as long as it deals with styles of worship and methods of education. They are much less certain about the applicability of the principle of inculturation—or the parallel need to be sensitive to cultural diversity—when the issue concerns the larger social context in which they function, rather than the internal arena of church doctrine or practice. Churches no doubt are not really conscious of doing an injustice to women and might well point out that women play important roles in the life of most congregations. On the other hand, the fact that certain roles seem to be implicitly off-limits on the basis of gender and that there seems to be some inequality in compensation for the taking on of comparable roles certainly raises some questions about how important "women's roles" are likely ever to be.

Questions for Group Discussion

1. To the extent that they can be separated for purposes of discussion, which issue do you think is the more important in understanding the situation in which Ms. Jamerson finds herself: the implicit gender discrimination in hiring and compensation policies at the church, or the church's violation of the principle of truly open, democratic decision making?

2. To what extent can we consider the current American preference for equal opportunity for each gender as a matter of *culture*? In other words,

does it resonate with longstanding beliefs and values that are consistent with and integrated into a general system of American beliefs and values and that are reasonably widely shared throughout the society—or is it simply a matter of passing political fashion?

3. Do you agree with the advice of any group of Ms. Jamerson's friends? If so, which ones? Why? If not, which ones? Why not? Can you think of any alternative advice not represented by her friends that you think she should follow?

4. Discuss the argument of those who point out logical, particularistic reasons for the church's practices as against a general policy of gender discrimination. Do you think Ms. Jamerson has an issue even if these specific cases are as they have been explained? If you were in her place, what would you want to find out before reaching a conclusion?

5. How do you assess the argument that even if the church's policies are discriminatory, they are still defensible because the church need not conform to the values of secular society?

6. Do you think that Ms. Jamerson's status as a political candidate should have any bearing on her interpretation of the case or on any decision she might make about it? Why or why not?

7. What resolution does your discussion group think would best serve Ms. Jamerson's individual needs as well as the long-term interest of the church community?

8. Discuss an example of possible gender discrimination in your own congregation or community. Which *cultural* factors might help you understand that problem? In what ways does your situation differ from the one at Taylor Road United Methodist? In what ways is it similar? How would your recommendation to your own group differ from the one you offered to Taylor Road? How would it be similar?

11

A CASE STUDY IN SEXUAL ORIENTATION

The Case Study

Dennis McKinley is a professional social worker who has for many years volunteered as the coordinator of a youth softball league in which most of the churches in his town participate. He has recently come out as a gay man and has confided to several close friends at Grace Lutheran, his own church, that he is HIV positive. He has been heartened by the genuine warmth of the personal support he has received from both the clergy and lay members of the community who know about his problem, and he was pleased when he was encouraged to start a support group for HIV-positive people that meets in his church's social hall on a weekly basis. On the other hand, he was deeply hurt when his pastor suggested to him that it would be best for all concerned if he withdrew from his softball league activities, since the parents were bound to find out that he is both gay and HIV positive and would certainly object to his working with the youngsters. The pastor assures Dennis that there will always be a place for him personally at Grace Lutheran, but at the same time vetoed his proposal to put on a series of AIDS-awareness workshops for members of the congregation. The pastor wants the members of the support group to understand that the church is simply providing meeting space—it is not going to turn into a "gay church" or an "AIDS church."

Mr. McKinley believes that he is being forced into a kind of religious ghetto because of both his sexual preference and his medical condition—allowed to participate in some aspects of church life, but excluded from others, even though he has always provided exemplary service and has given no one the slightest reason to question his work with the kids. He has come to feel that expressions of concern for him personally (or for the other members of his support group) are meaningless unless he is allowed to play a full role in the community. He does not want to make a political issue about his status, but neither does he want Grace Lutheran to put such a narrow construction on its exercise of charity and compassion. He knows that he could join the local Metropolitan Community Church, which serves an avowedly gay congregation, but he feels strongly that Grace Lutheran has been his church ever since he moved to the city and he should be allowed to continue being a member there as he always has been, in spite of what people now know about his personal life.

Discussion and Analysis

Moral theologians in most Christian traditions agree that while homosexual acts may be considered sinful, the basic "orientation" toward homosexuality is not. It is, however, by no means clear in the scientific literature whether sexual orientation per se is an inherent (i.e., genetically patterned) matter or whether it is learned behavior. It is, on the other hand, quite clear that the sorts of behaviors adopted by people who self-identify with a given sexual preference (in this case, homosexuality) are learned in the context of culture. The question here, then, should be whether Mr. McKinley has exhibited within the community *learned behaviors* that the community finds incompatible with its own values.

The hysterical charges that AIDS is a form of divine punishment for unacceptable lifestyles have more or less abated, but there are still many who feel that certain people "brought it on themselves" because of their choices. But the same could be said about people who smoke, fail to eat a healthy diet or exercise regularly, and so forth, and who therefore "bring on" cancer, heart disease, and other ailments—although that charge does not have the same moral connotations that are typical of discussions of HIV disease. The fact is that AIDS is an infectious disease that is *facilitated* by certain lifestyle choices, but is not caused by them. In other countries, AIDS is predominantly a disease of married heterosexuals; in some communities women are at higher risk than men, and in some cases there is particularly high incidence among children. The disease is caused by a virus that, in the manner of all viruses, simply seeks the most opportune avenue to propagate itself. Whatever other moral judgments we may make about homosexuality (or about intravenous drug use, for that matter, another risk factor in HIV infection in our society), it is simply incorrect to conclude that AIDS is somehow the unique and inevitable outcome of that lifestyle.

Mr. McKinley's case, however, raises some difficult questions for the proponent of cultural diversity. Most people of good will agree that it is morally (as well as socially and politically) desirable to foster tolerance for members of other racial or ethnic groups and socioeconomic classes, for women, for old people, and for people with disabilities. Nonmainstream sexual orientation, by contrast, is the only major category of social differentiation that is morally stigmatized, such that even people of good will might well ask why they should try to accommodate themselves to a group that chooses to practice and defend activities that are considered fundamentally improper. Even if people were willing to be tolerant on philosophical grounds, and even if Mr. McKinley never did anything improper around the youth, people might still wonder, rightly or wrongly, whether they need to tolerate someone who defends the homosexual lifestyle in a situation that brings him into close contact with impressionable youngsters. And even if all the moral questions are set aside, people without complete and up-to-date medical information might wonder if there were not some possibility that an accidental cut or other unintended physical contact with someone who is HIV positive could be harmful to the children.

Grace Lutheran seems to have made a concession to society at large by allowing its facilities to serve as a meeting place for a stigmatized minority. But what are its obligations to those people beyond that allowance?

Questions for Group Discussion

1. Given the suggestion that AIDS is a viral disease that is facilitated, but not caused by, certain social practices, how might Grace Lutheran (and, by extension, the other churches that participate in the softball league) go about finding out about the specific nature of the AIDS epidemic in its local culture? What do you think of the pastor's refusal to take Mr. McKinley up on his offer to present an informational workshop?

2. How does this case illustrate the potential conflict between "ideal" culture (i.e., what people think they *should* do) and "real" culture (what they actually do)?

3. Evaluate the pros and cons of allowing Mr. McKinley to continue his volunteer work with the softball league. Doing so will require you to balance the rights of the individual against the rights of the community. Come up with recommended courses of action for Mr. McKinley, for Grace Lutheran, for the parents of the kids who play in the league, for clergy and

lay members of the other churches involved in the league. Do these recommendations harmonize with one another, or do some contradict others? If the latter, how do you prioritize the needs that must be addressed?

4. Discuss a case in which sexual orientation has become an issue in your own community. Which *cultural* factors differentiate your community from that described in this case. Which ones are similar? How would you recommend resolving the issue in your community? Is (are) your solution(s) different or the same from the ones you recommended in the case of Mr. McKinley? If so, why? If not, why not?

12

A CASE STUDY IN AGING

The Case Study

The members of the community service group at the Harborside Church of Christ have decided to develop an outreach program for the residents of Shady Acres, a large retirement community in their part of the city. Larry Preston and Nancy Pratt are coordinating this effort and have presented a plan to the board of trustees. They recommend establishing a special worship service at 8 A.M. with the senior citizens in mind. They point out that people with families generally don't get organized to get out that early, whereas older people are frequently up at that hour. The younger families would still go to the main service, at 10:30. The eight o'clock service would feature old, familiar hymns, and the minister would be reminded to stay at the pulpit when preaching and not go wandering around like a talk-show host, as he has a tendency to do at the more modern services.

In addition to the special worship service, Mr. Preston and Ms. Pratt are recommending that a seniors' club be formed to cater to both the social and spiritual interests of the Shady Acres group. They have lined up a series of interesting lecturers from the community college who will address the seniors on a variety of topics including health care, financial planning, Broadway musicals, and local archaeology. A retired minister from a nearby church has agreed to lead a special Bible study for members of the seniors' club. Members of the youth group will be encouraged to pay regular visits to the old folks, and the men's club will be asked to provide transportation for the seniors who can no longer drive themselves to meetings or services. The children's program will begin an "adopt-a-grandparent" project for the holiday season.

Discussion and Analysis

At first glance, this case study doesn't seem to fit the pattern of the others presented thus far, in that there doesn't really seem to be a problem. The Harborside Church appears to be a model of enlightened outreach to its senior citizen neighbors, and the members of the church seem to have gone more than the proverbial extra mile in accommodating the diversity represented by this particular population.

On the other hand, Mr. Preston and Ms. Pratt have made some fundamental errors that may doom the program, carefully planned and well intended though it is. Recall that it is always advisable to get the "insiders' perspective" when analyzing a given social situation. That piece of advice was offered in the context of going beyond the one "spokesman" who put himself forward on behalf of the group in the Riverdale Community case, but in the Harborside case, not only was there a suspect "spokesperson"—there was *no* spokesperson at all. Larry and Nancy certainly would not have acted as they did if they were trying to open the church to members of a racial or ethnic minority because they would not have assumed that they knew enough about the group to make plans for them. They almost certainly would have asked *somebody* for advice. But we tend to assume that we know all about old age because it's part of our common experience. It is certainly true that most of the initiatives recommended by Larry and Nancy conform to our stereotypes about what older people prefer in the way of both worship styles and social activities.

But nobody ever bothered to find out! There isn't even any direct evidence that any of the Shady Acres residents were interested in having closer relations with Harborside Church. Seeking the insider perspective is fundamental to any question of diversity. After all, if we really already knew what every group needed and wanted, there wouldn't be an issue of "cultural diversity" at all—"they" would already be "us."

The net effect of all the good intentions at Harborside is that Larry and Nancy have created a kind of glorified ghetto. They have gone so far in the direction of accommodating the seniors and creating "special" programs for them, that they have, in effect, defined them out of the mainstream life of the congregation. Whatever else "healthy aging" might mean, it almost certainly does not include allowing seniors to be treated as helpless, voiceless, passive recipients of their juniors' charity. Within reason, it is possible for older people to "take charge" of their aging, as the social gerontology literature has pointed out.

It is not inconceivable that a planning and evaluation process that includes the Shady Acres residents would come up with pretty much the same set of programs that Mr. Preston and Ms. Pratt have already recommended. But a population that is "ministered to" is never really a part of the same community in the same way that a population that has taken some ownership of ministry can be said to be. In effect, the content of the seniors' programs might in the long run be less important than the value of including them in the decision-making process to begin with.

Questions for Group Discussion

1. Review the five "tasks" of healthy aging discussed earlier. How might these apply to the people living at Shady Acres and worshiping at Harborside Church?

2. Would it make any difference if we knew more about other aspects of the Shady Acres community? For example, are most of the residents white or black—and how does the racial/ethnic composition of the retirement community compare with that of the church? How many of the senior citizens are disabled in some way? What is their socioeconomic status—and how does it compare with the average status of the members of the church? Are most of them longtime residents of the neighborhood who have only recently moved into retirement housing, or are they people who have relocated from far away? (In other words, do they have their own preexisting social networks in the city, or are they isolated within the retirement community?)

3. In what ways does this case illustrate the potential conflict between "ideal" culture (what people think they *ought* to do) and "real" culture (what they actually end up doing)?

4. How would you advise Mr. Preston and Ms. Pratt to go about securing an insiders' perspective for their planning efforts? The answer should involve more than simply saying, "Get a Shady Acres resident to join the panel." You will need to be more specific: How many residents? how are they to be selected? will it be a matter of one person, one vote, or will the senior citizens have some sort of veto power over decisions affecting their participation?

5. Discuss a case in your own community in which aging has been an important issue. Has the response been to treat older people as a population to be ministered to, or have they been integrated in other ways into the community life?

13

A CASE STUDY IN DISABILITY AND COMMUNITY

The Case Study

The Otis T. McBrien Foundation supports residential options for adults with mental and physical disabilities who are unable to live fully independent lives. The foundation is endowed by parents. Funds are then used to build state-of-the-art group homes. Adults with disabilities who have always been cared for by their parents are thereby assured of having a good place to live once their parents pass away or are otherwise no longer capable of caring for them. A fundamental part of the McBrien philosophy is that the group homes are built on property donated by churches, so that there will be an ongoing relationship between the medical and physical care of the group home residents and the spiritual aspects of their lives. In the city where the foundation first operated, group homes have already been built on Roman Catholic, Presbyterian, and Methodist properties. A new facility is being planned at St. Cyril Greek Orthodox Church.

Father Michael Vastos, the pastor, is taking the lead to make sure that the church is prepared to welcome the residents. He has brought in a contractor to make sure that there are ramps leading into both the church proper and the parish hall, that the aisles of the church are wide enough to accommodate wheelchairs, and that all the rest rooms are wheelchair accessible. A special section has been reserved for the hearing impaired at every service, and a signer trained at the local college has been assigned. Large-print editions of the hymnal and prayer book are available on request for those with visual impairments. Special Bible study classes have been arranged for those with mental retardation. The church has also agreed to buy a van and hire a driver to transport the residents to the various sheltered workshops where they work during the week. The youth group will be encouraged to develop a "buddy" program with the residents so that they can be included in various social events at the church.

Discussion and Analysis

This case is very similar to that of the senior outreach program at Harborside Church. Once again we have a church that has really gone out of its way to provide a respectful and welcoming atmosphere for a group that enhances the overall diversity of the community, in this case people with disabilities. Once again we have an array of programs and services that, on the face of it, seem to be beyond criticism—they are precisely what any sensible person would think is appropriate.

But once again we find that the principal players have violated a cardinal rule in the application of the culture principle: All the plans are "outsider"-generated. There is no indication at all of any representative of the foundation (let alone of the residents themselves) being asked what they need or want, nor is there any indication that their opinions are being built into the ongoing development plans. This lapse is perhaps even more disturbing here than it was in the previous case; senior citizens, at least, have available to them well-organized advocacy groups through which they can make their opinions heard. But people with disabilities have long labored under a system in which the advocacy groups are really the voices of the caretakers, rarely of the people with disabilities themselves. Part of the empowerment of people with disabilities has been the assumption that they can (and should, and must) be allowed to speak for their own interests. The St. Cyril's initiatives, extremely well intended (and probably very effective and appreciated as well) though they are, neglected to take into account what is perhaps the most salient aspect of disability in the United States—the tendency to shut the disabled out of effective decision-making roles.

There is a further problem at St. Cyril's: Although Father Vastos and his staff have apparently made every effort to meet the needs of people with various kinds of disabilities, there is still a tendency to treat the whole issue as a kind of "disabled outreach" effort. In effect, "the disabled" have been ghettoized by identifying the McBrien residents solely on the basis of their disabilities. One gets the sense that people with various impairments are "accommodated" by the church only in terms of their special needs. There is not much sense that they are otherwise integrated into the life of the community. Remember that disability is relational—it is always defined relative to some particular community in which particular roles need to be carried out; it should not be thought of in absolute terms. But at St. Cyril, the only operative relationship seems to be "disabled" versus "everyone else." There is not much emphasis placed on what people with disabilities are able to do in the context of the church community—only on what they need to have done for them.

Questions for Group Discussion

1. Think about the abilities of "disabled" people. What sorts of roles in a church community might people with hearing or visual or cognitive or physical impairment be able to play? (In other words, think beyond what the congregation can do to compensate for these peoples' deficits; think in terms of what the people can positively contribute to the life of the church in general.)

2. Discuss the pros and cons of considering HIV-positive status as a "disability" instead of a factor of sexual orientation, as in a previous case study. What about age as a disability?

3. Do you think that people with disabilities think of their conditions as the prime source of their self-identification—or are they more likely to make common cause with other, "abled" people of their own race, ethnic group, gender, socioeconomic class, sexual orientation, or age category? Which of these criteria do you think is *generally* the most important? Which do you think is the most important in the McBrien-St. Cyril setting? How would you find out what the actual situation is?

4. Devise a plan for incorporating an insiders' perspective in the planning process at St. Cyril's. (Remember that doing so should involve more than simply advocating adding disabled people to the relevant committees. Discuss how such people would be chosen and what specific roles they would play.)

5. Discuss a situation in your own community in which disability seems to have played an important role. Were the disabled treated primarily as objects of the community's charity, or were they integrated into the community in a more positive way? What particular *cultural* factors in your community make it different from the situation at St. Cyril's? In what ways are they similar?

14

A CASE STUDY IN RACIAL ATTITUDES

The Case Study

St. Luke Episcopal Church operates one of the most successful private academies in the state. Its students have for the past decade ranked near the top in test scores, and many have been admitted to the most prestigious colleges. Although students are selected on the basis of academic merit, and need not be affiliated with the church, the academy's board of governors feels that the values derived from the Episcopalian traditions of open inquiry, discipline, community, and commitment to scholarship have given the school its scholastic edge.

One of the academy's former governors was Nicholas Rodney, whose family had for decades operated several businesses in the city's old downtown area, now a largely African American neighborhood. Mr. Rodney, who was eager to give black youth a helping hand, passed away a few years ago, leaving in his will a sizeable bequest to St. Luke's Academy. The funds were earmarked as scholarships for inner-city students. This year, three black students began classes at the academy.

While most members of the church and the school administration were publicly enthusiastic about the new scholarship program, several of them privately expressed serious doubts. There was a feeling that although the school had in the past admitted many students whose families were not affiliated with the church, they had never had to deal with students from such a vastly different cultural background. The three students seemed to have good academic records, but after all they had been at extremely underresourced schools—their ability to keep up with students who had come to St. Luke's from top-notch schools in more affluent neighborhoods was very much in doubt. Some parents said that while the three students seemed nice enough, they came from an environment in which violence, drug abuse, and family dysfunction were all too common—how long would it be before their true nature emerged?

Matters reached a crisis point when a white student reported that she had been accosted in a hallway near the cafeteria. The assailant had been scared away when some other people came down the hall, but she was sure that he had a knife and that he intended to drag her outside into an alley and rape her. The girl was unable to identify her attacker, but the rumor soon spread that one of the scholarship students had been the mugger. The young man was summoned to the principal's office, where he seemed sullen and uncooperative, so much so that he was suspended on the spot. His parents angrily charged the school with racism and have hired a lawyer to press their case. A group of white parents, in retaliation, have demanded that the school simply return the Rodney bequest and end the scholarship program. No good, they say, can ever come of mixing incompatible social groups. Mr. Rodney had been a very good, idealistic man, but he was naive to think that his little experiment in social engineering would come to anything but grief.

Discussion and Analysis

This case illustrates how in America the old demon of racialist thinking can undo even the best intended, most progressive social initiatives, although not always in the most obvious, stereotypical ways. Some might say, for example, that Mr. Rodney himself had been guilty of racialist thinking, since he designated his scholarship funds for African American youth. On the other hand, he clearly parted company with classic racists in his belief that the problems of African American youth were not biologically inherited, but the result of unfavorable social circumstances, which could be undone by a proper education. In a similar way, the parents who are demanding an end to the program are basing their argument not on classic racist logic, but on an odd kind of cultural awareness: It is the difference in culture between the inner city and the more affluent neighborhoods that is the issue, not *race* in the old-fashioned sense of that term. The parents of the suspended student, on the other hand, seem to be responding out of a long experience of frustration with uncomprehending white authority figures—their unspoken assumption is that a white student who had been less than polite to the principal would have been cut some slack and would not have been dismissed out of hand as a hopeless case.

It is important to keep in mind that the behavior that gets the black student in trouble is, in this context, rather subtle. It is actually quite understandable that as a newcomer to the school, where he is in a very visible minority position, the young man was very nervous upon being summoned to the principal's office. And he reacted with justifiable anger at being questioned about the ugly incident when there is no indication that any of the white students were thought to be involved. And yet his understandable psychological reaction to the situation seemed to conform to the St. Luke's community's stereotypes about what people from the inner city were like. This sort of reasoning is sometimes referred to as the "ecological fallacy"—the assumption that any individual member of a defined social group exhibits all of the characteristics presumed to be typical of the group in general. In other cases in this workbook, we have seen the difficulty inherent in assuming that one individual represents an entire group; here we see the problems of burdening the individual with the traits of a group (which has been painted in stereotypical colors to begin with).

Questions for Group Discussion

1. Leaving aside technical legal matters raised by the parents' lawsuit, what do you see as the most important issues raised by this case?

2. White parents, white students, black parents, black students, the school authorities, the church authorities, the executors of the Rodney estate— these are all potential stakeholders in the crisis at St. Luke. Drawing on your understanding of the various aspects of our understanding of culture, carefully describe their respective interests in the problem. Do you think that they represent incompatible interests? If not, where do you see common ground?

3. Can you think of any ways in which the problem might have been avoided before it ever reached a crisis point? Is there anything that could be done to avoid having similar things happen in the future? What can you suggest to the St. Luke community in general by way of resolving the current conflict?

4. Can you think of any cases analogous to this one that have occurred in your own community? If so, how was it resolved? If it has not yet been resolved, what have you learned from studying this case that might help you understand your own situation a little better?

15

A CASE STUDY IN LANGUAGE AS SOCIAL CAPITAL

The Case Study

The international airport serving a major metropolitan area offers an extensive chaplaincy program. Qualified ministers representing most of the local Christian denominations are on duty in regular rotation. They provide counseling and referral services to travelers and also conduct nondenominational worship services on Sundays and holidays, as well as more informal prayer services during the week. The program is coordinated by Helen Gray, a layperson whose salary is covered jointly by the participating churches. Ms. Gray is responsible for arranging the ministers' schedules and for the upkeep of the small airport chapel. She also talks informally to confused or lonely people who are unable or unwilling to wait for one of the ministers, although she is always careful to remind them that she is "just a friendly face" and is not certified to offer either psychological counseling or spiritual direction.

Ms. Gray is an extremely hardworking and unfailingly cheerful and courteous representative of the chaplaincy program, in particular, and, indeed, of the airport, in general. Everyone agrees that her "just a friendly face" conversations are often more useful and more gratefully received than are formal counseling sessions with a recognized authority figure. When notice was received of a national conference of airport chaplaincy program officers, most of the ministers assumed that Ms. Gray would be commissioned as their airport's representative. A few of their colleagues, however, raised some quiet objections.

The problem, as the dissenters see it, is that Ms. Gray "does not project the right image" required at such an august gathering. You see, Ms. Gray is not only not an ordained minister or a counselor with a degree—she is without higher education of any kind and earned a high school equivalency diploma while serving a sentence in prison. It was there that she met one of the ministers, who divides his time between serving the prison and the airport, and who, impressed with Ms. Gray's good will and capacity for hard work, recommended her for the airport coordinator's position. There was some initial skepticism, although by now everyone is convinced that Ms. Gray has paid her debt to society and has no lingering criminal tendencies. But her speech patterns are, in the words of one of the ministers, "crude and nearly illiterate." Her lack of pretension may work well when she is "just a friendly face" to strangers, but her linguistic incompetence would be nothing but an embarrassment were she to represent the airport at a prestigious national conference.

Some of the other ministers agreed that until you get to know her, Ms. Gray can come off as a bit of a dunce because of her poor grammar and often incorrect choice of words. Her malapropisms can seem amusing to those who already know and trust her, but she does take a bit of getting used to. Is this really the image this airport and this chaplaincy program want to present to the outside world? They suggested a compromise: a delegation, rather than a single representative, would go to the conference, and one of the professionals would take care of any public presentations, leaving Ms. Gray to do what she does best—make friends in small, private meetings. The minister who sponsored Ms. Gray, however, was incensed. He had no objection to sending a larger delegation if the money could be found, but he thought it would be an insult to keep Ms. Gray—who, after all, was the only one who really knew how the program worked and whose insights would be of greatest value to the conferees at large—from participating fully in the conference proceedings.

What began as a quiet disagreement among the ministers has thus become something of a heated argument. One side points out that surely for Christians the measure of a person is what is in her or his heart and not something as superficial as how she or he speaks. The other side claims that how one speaks is not a superficial matter at all, that even Christians are responsible for the images they project to the world at large, and that in any case they needed to be concerned about the image of their airport and their city, and not just of themselves as Christians. It proved impossible to keep the debate from Ms. Gray. When she heard about it, she told the ministers that she would offer to resign if they could come up with someone more worthy to represent them. In order to avert that resolution, her main supporter offered to give her an intensive set of speech lessons, but Ms. Gray took this as a further insult and decided to resign on the spot.

Discussion and Analysis

While we might like to think that we treat all people on their individual mer-its—a good, general, democratic American principle as well as a Christian one—the fact is that the impressions people make influence the way we deal with them. The way we speak is inevitably an important element in the kind of image we project, since speech is the primary way in which we communi-cate and share. Language is, after all, the vehicle for the transmission of cul-ture. Whatever impedes the easy interchange of ideas and impressions thereby sets up cultural barriers that make for sometimes unexpected barri-ers exaggerating the effects of diversity. The way we use language gives oth-ers a great deal of symbolic information about our social class, age, gender, and perhaps even our racial or ethnic group and sexual orientation. That in-formation may, in fact, be wrong, but we need to be conscious of the messages we give and receive in order to get past them to the "real people" beneath the symbolic overlay.

In this situation, the fact that the people discussing Ms. Gray's qualifications to represent the program knew something about her background probably made them interpret the symbolic information conveyed by her speech in more negative ways than might otherwise have been the case. Since they already knew she had been in prison and was not well educated, it was easy enough to exag-gerate the effects that her rough language might have on others. It is conceivable that had they known nothing about her, they would have judged her crude lan-guage as just an unfortunate lapse. And if they had been introduced to her as the coordinator of a major program, they might have assumed her to be a highly ed-ucated person who had simply adopted a "low-class" way of speaking as some sort of odd affectation—an extreme example, perhaps, of the tendency of politi-cians to drop their g's and throw in a few "ain'ts" to demonstrate their solidarity with the masses. But, unfortunately for Ms. Gray, they did have that other in-formation, suspicions about which could only be confirmed by her speech pat-terns. It seems that even her staunchest defender was put off or embarrassed by her language since he offered to give her special tutoring to overcome the defect. He obviously knew that language, which is a cultural trait, is learned behavior, and thus can be unlearned or relearned as circumstances require. What he failed to recognize, however, is that how one speaks is not a neutral cultural element, but one that carries enormous "symbolic capital" both for society at large and for individual speakers. Ms. Gray might not have been offended had the minister offered to help her learn to use a laptop computer so that she wouldn't have to take notes at the conference with pen and paper. In fact, she might have been pleased to learn a new skill. But the suggestion that her language needed im-provement struck a nerve. In effect, he wasn't saying that she needed to add a new skill to her repertoire; he was saying that there was something wrong with her as a person because she lacked a certain standard of behavior.

Ms. Gray, as an intelligent and sensitive person, probably realizes at some level that her speech is considered "substandard" and would indeed cause her to stand out in a negative way in the context of the professional conference. But we would want to know more about how she interprets the "symbolic capital" involved in this situation. Does she really want to advance her professional career, perhaps getting a degree in counseling at some point? If so, she might be willing to take whatever steps were necessary to acquire more acceptable speech patterns. But perhaps she is happy doing what she does now as a friendly nonprofessional and only wants to participate in this one conference because she has the expertise and background to make a real contribution to its deliberations. Should she submit to a major renovation of her personal inventory just to accommodate a one-time situation and to please a group of people she will probably never have to interact with again? Keep in mind that while learned cultural behavior can, indeed, be unlearned or relearned, doing so is no easy matter. Changing the way we speak means, in effect, turning our backs on how we presented ourselves for a long period of time, and there have to be very significant incentives to engage in such a process.

Questions for Group Discussion

1. Who are the key players in this case study? What values or attitudes do you think account for their actions? To what extent are those values and attitudes the products of culture (as opposed to those that are individual/psychological)?

2. To what extent do you think that the negative evaluation of Ms. Gray's "symbolic capital" as expressed by her speech patterns was affected by other attributes? For example, is "rough talk" from a woman considered more inappropriate than similar talk from a man? Would we want to know more about Ms. Gray's relative age? her racial or ethnic affiliation? What difference would such information make?

   a. Would the situation have been different had Ms. Gray been a degreed professional who affected rough speech? In what ways? What kind of relationship between Ms. Gray and the ministers is implied by the various dimensions that define her status?

3. Which do you think is of greater importance in this case: the Christian (and basic American) principle of fair play and tolerance, or the pragmatic considerations of impression management in professional settings?

4. To what extent have the ministers prejudged the situation? In other words, have they identified a "problem" before ascertaining whether one

really exists? How could they be so sure that Ms. Gray's rough-hewn ways were going to turn off the other conference participants?

5. Since the minister's offer to give Ms. Gray speech lessons was taken as an insult, what might he have done instead if he were sincerely convinced that this was an aspect of her social demeanor that needed to be modified?

6. What impact does the social setting have on the dimensions of this case? For example, would the same questions have been raised had Ms. Gray been the administrative assistant at a small, local parish rather than in a large, public facility? Do you think it would have made a difference had a single local denomination been in charge of the airport chaplaincy program, as opposed to an ecumenical ministry?

7. What does the concept of "symbolic capital" mean to you (1) as a member of society at large? (2) as a Christian?

8. Based on your analysis of this case study, how would you advise the airport ministers to deal with Ms. Gray? Should they try to convince her to come back? How? If not, what responsibilities (if any) do they have toward her now that she is no longer working with them? If she does come back, how would you propose to handle the question of the conference representation? (Answer that question both as a short-term issue, one that affects this one conference at this time, and as a long-term matter, one that might come up again if the conference becomes a permanent consortium of airport ministerial programs.)

9. What lessons have you learned from your analysis of the airport ministry that could apply to a situation in your own congregation or community? In what ways does your situation differ from that of the airport? In what ways are the situations similar? Which *cultural* factors might need to be considered in coming up with a solution to the specific problems of your own community?

16

A CASE STUDY IN FAMILY ORGANIZATION

The Case Study

The United Community Church serves a small, but very active congregation in a medium-sized city. Of its many activities, it is proudest of its innovative "Moms' Club," a program of Bible study, group sharing, and community service held at the same time that the moms' kids are in Bible study classes of their own. The members of the Moms' Club all say that the group has enabled them to forge strong and lasting friendships. It has also given them a firm grounding in current biblical scholarship that enables them to carry out their service projects in what they believe to be a truly Christian spirit.

The members of the club were taken aback, however, when Josh Tiller showed up at one of their meetings and asked to join. Josh is a single dad who adopted his son Jake after the death of his wife. He explains,

> Marnie and I always wanted children, but she was too ill most of the time for us to consider it. Then after she passed on, I thought, "Well, why wait until I get married again? Who knows when, or if that will happen? But I still want a child. I do most of my business by telecommuting, so I'm home most of the time anyway. I think I can be a good parent." So I went through the adoption process. Jake was five years old when he came to live with me. He had some medical problems, but we're dealing with them and now he's doing great.

The women in the club all like Josh and wish him and Jake well, but they decided by an overwhelming vote to ask him not to join their group.

Fran Talbott, the president of the club, spoke to Josh privately, and explained, as gently as she could, the members' reasons. First, she said, the basis of the friendship bonds that were so important to them was the fact that all the members were women and felt comfortable sharing with each other in ways that would be almost impossible if a man were part of the discussion. Some of the women would be inclined to keep their opinions to themselves and to defer to a man, while others would be too embarrassed to talk about personal matters in his presence. Fran suggested that perhaps he help out the church by volunteering to coach the soccer team instead of by joining the Moms' Club. Josh responded by pointing out that while he certainly couldn't do anything about being a man, the fact is that he was playing the same functional role as all the women in the club—the home-based caregiver to a young child. He thought that on that basis he had far more in common with them than they might at first realize, in spite of his gender. He would be happy to help out the soccer team, but he said that his main concern was becoming an effective, faith-filled parent—something he thought he could accomplish better in the club than on the athletic field.

Fran then turned to the members' second objection. While the women hoped Josh and Jake were happy and healthy, they felt that they couldn't condone Josh's unconventional lifestyle choice, which did not seem to be in keeping with the church's teachings about the family. They meant no offense, she added quickly, and did not mean to judge either his actions or his motives, but neither did they want to give the community at large the impression that they approved what he had done. It would be different if Jake were the child of Josh and his late wife and he was now facing life as a widowed father. But under the circumstances, it could seem that Josh had adopted the boy to satisfy the selfish need to fill a void in his life after his wife's passing. It was something, she said, that you might expect of some movie star, but not something that could be a model for people in a nice, middle-class community.

Josh was surprised at the bluntness of Fran's comments, which were delivered in polite tones but which, he felt, carried a harsh, indeed an un-Christian message. He told her that he and Marnie had always felt very comfortable at United Community and that Jake was making good friends among the other children in his Bible class. Josh did not think it was fair to deprive him of the opportunity to continue to enjoy community and fellowship of his own, just because he had made an unorthodox choice. "There's nothing either illegal or immoral about what I did," he said. Fran agreed, but added, "But you have to remember that we're out there in the community carrying the name of this church. Just by virtue of the fact that you'd be the only man working on our projects, you'd be very visible, and it would seem as if your choice were one we'd all endorse." Josh countered that just allowing him to join needn't be considered an endorsement, and he thought that Pastor Francis would back him up on that count, but Fran said that the membership was united in the decision, and she begged him not to embarrass the church by making a big public hassle over it.

Discussion and Analysis

The case of the man and the Moms' Club can be analyzed first against the backdrop of some of the demographic figures reported earlier. For one thing we learned that the number of households composed of men with children but without a woman in residence has risen dramatically from twelve million to thirty-two million in the past twenty years. That is still a minority of households in the United States, but it is a number sufficiently large as to lead us to the conclusion that this situation is not a fringe anomaly. Of course, the numbers themselves do not give us a complete picture. For one thing, the figures as reported do not distinguish families headed by widowers or divorced men raising children from their marriages from those headed by single men raising children incorporated into the household by other means. The likelihood is that the latter will still be a minority within the minority. But this minitrend toward single-male-headed households must be seen in the larger context reported previously, which demonstrates quite clearly that it is one of several formerly nonstandard family organizations that have now collectively become the norm. It is the familiar two-parent nuclear family that is the real minority.

These demographic issues, however, must be fleshed out by attention to what is happening to real people in real communities. The fact that something has become statistically normative does not mean that it needs to be viewed as desirable. In this case under consideration here, the church (as opposed, for example, to a public school) would seem to be an appropriate place to insert the question of the relative value of different forms of family in the moral sense. On the other hand, moral standards often follow in the wake of strong demographic trends— divorce, considered a shocking aberration or the affectation of show business celebrities not so many decades ago, is now so common that it rarely evokes comment, let alone moral disapproval.[1] Perhaps other formerly nonstandard forms of the family will come to enjoy the same privileged "no-comment" status.

Morality, however, has other dimensions, when it comes to the question of "family values." For example, it is probably safe to assume that everyone agrees that good parenting must involve spending "quality time" with children. In this case, Josh is fortunate in having the sort of job that allows him to spend a great deal of time with his son. And the fact that he is eager to place his relationship with the boy in the context of a wholesome church community suggests that he is sincere in his efforts to maximize the quality of the time they spend together. On the other hand, some might suggest that in having deliberately chosen to raise Jake in a single-parent household, Josh has forfeited some claims to the quality-time high ground. Has he not deprived Jake of the benefits of a stable two-parent home? Are there not things that a mother can give to a child that even the most sensitive and caring father cannot? Can any single parent, of either gender, really be all things to a child?

Questions for Group Discussion

1. The moms give two main reasons for asking Josh not to join their group. Carefully consider both these arguments from the standpoint of current social and demographic research. Do these arguments carry equivalent weight for you? Do you think they carry equivalent weight in the thinking of the moms at United Community?

2. We do not know what specific church teachings are involved in the moms' hesitation to approve Josh's lifestyle choice, but from the standpoint of your own community's beliefs, how would you evaluate the morality of his family organization? Do you think that the moms have a right to insert the question of morality into this discussion? Does a "truly Christian" attitude require us to accept everybody on his or her own terms?

3. Do you think it would have made a difference to the moms had the newcomer been a single woman with an adopted child? If so, why? If not, why not?

4. How would you advise the United Community moms to deal with Josh?

5. Can you think of analogous cases in your own community? If so, how could they best be handled? Is the advice you give to your own community the same or different from the advice you would give to United Community? Explain the similarities or differences.

17

A CASE STUDY IN INTERFAITH COOPERATION

The Case Study

Nearly a decade ago, a group of dedicated laypeople in a large city banded together to form an organization known as the Christian Coalition. It includes representatives of most of the mainstream denominations that have a large presence in the city, as well as several smaller independent community churches. The coalition was formed to "foster interfaith dialogue," but the participants quickly realized that the dialogue had a tendency to bog down on points of theology and styles of prayer and worship that were the result of centuries of divergent development. Such issues, they saw, certainly could not be resolved by a few meetings of local churches. So the group decided that, rather than haggle over philosophical nuances, they would unite around a principle all Christians could certainly agree on—the call to help the poor. They decided to jointly sponsor a program to deal with the homeless population of the city, in the hope that a cooperative effort on behalf of a shared social commitment would do more to bring together people of different faith traditions than any number of discussion forums.

Over the years the Coalition Center has developed into a major service program. The first element was a soup kitchen, followed by a small emergency shelter, a job-referral service, and an after-school program for children. The center is considered a model of its kind and has been the recipient of numerous grants in aid of its programs. Local, state, and even national politicians typically make it a point to be photographed at the center whenever they visit the city, and they consistently praise it as an example of constructive volunteer effort.

As the center has grown, however, several issues have arisen that threaten to divert the attention of its participants from its fundamental mission. First, there has been considerable talk about the need to "professionalize" the program. From its inception, the center has been both administered and staffed by volunteers, but as the program has grown in scope and reputation, there has been a perceived need to hire full-time managers, financial officers, grant writers, social workers, and so forth. Some of the founders argue that professionalizing the center would destroy its original vision; the point all along was for members of different church communities to learn about each other by working together, a sense that would be lost if most of the activities were placed in the hands of paid professionals whose ties to the churches (and to the Christian message the center embodied) would be tenuous as best. Others disagree, however, pointing out that well-intentioned volunteers simply do not have the expertise (or, for that matter, the time) to run a large and complex organization in ways that are fiscally sound and conform to all sorts of government requirements mandated for such facilities. The program, they contend, will collapse under its own weight unless competent full-time professionals take charge. This group claims that, after all, most churches, even relatively small ones, have professional staffs of one sort or another—they rarely can survive by relying exclusively on volunteers— and the larger ones have evolved into fairly complex bureaucracies over the years, without doing essential damage to their Christian vision.

A second issue concerns the kind of Christianity involved in the provision of services at the center. One group feels that simply doing works widely recognized as beneficial is ample evidence of the Christian nature of the project. Others, however, point out that plenty of secular agencies do works equally good; if the center is to be a truly Christian enterprise, it must be more active in presenting the Word of God to the people it serves. They propose that Bible study classes be mandatory for people receiving meals at the soup kitchen and that regular worship services be required for those staying at the shelter for any extended period of time. The children in the after-school program, they say, ought to be involved in activities that are geared explicitly to the learning of Christian principles.

Still a third bone of contention has been the nature of the population to be served. Homelessness, after all, is a phenomenon with many different faces. Homeless people are black and white, men and women, and of various ethnic backgrounds. They represent most age groups and probably all shades of sexual orientation. One segment of the homeless population is composed of people temporarily down on their luck who mainly need an opportunity to find decent jobs so that they can move into housing of their own. Another group consists of people who might be considered chronically homeless—most often people with mental or other disabilities who will probably never be able to hold down the kinds of jobs that would allow them to get off the streets. And then there are those who are, in effect, voluntarily homeless—people who simply prefer a lifestyle unfettered by normal social conventions. These distinctions are further crosscut by lines separating those who are longtime residents of the city from those who are just passing through. Single men, single women, couples with children, and couples without children all have distinctive service needs. One segment of the center's workers feels strongly that the program ought to serve whoever comes to its door. Another group believes that the center will be more effective if it targets its services—selects only one or two segments of the very diverse homeless population and gears its efforts to their specific needs, rather than trying to be all things to all people. Still another segment believes that waiting for walk-ins of any kind is self-defeating—it is necessary to go out to the highway underpasses, the freight yards, the patches of woods where homeless people typically camp, and bring people to the center, whose services they might not otherwise hear about or think were appropriate for them. A fourth group advocates for reserving services for those whose attitudes reaffirm the Christian message—in other words, excluding people with nonstandard sexual orientations, unmarried women with children, and so forth.

Discussion and Analysis

Many of the themes treated separately elsewhere in this book converge in this case study, which was deliberately structured for maximum complexity. The large issues of power and governance are involved in the debate over the staffing of the Coalition Center, while the familiar elements of cultural diversity—race, ethnicity, socioeconomic class, gender, age, disability, sexual orientation, language, family structure—are factors in the reappraisal of the center's service mission.

Underlying all these concerns in a much more direct way than has been typical of the other case studies is the question of the "Christian mission." The other cases were illustrated by one denomination or another (although the situations could occur in virtually any church community), so one could assume that the participants shared basic principles for the practice of their faith. The case study featuring Bigtime University placed Christians in a decision-making context that extended far beyond specifically Christian concerns. But this case is one in which Christianity in its most general form ("mere Christianity" in Lewis's phrase) itself becomes an issue. The coalition members consciously set aside the most obvious denominational differences reflected in theological interpretations or structures of worship and concentrated on what they presumed to be a common social value. The problem seems to be that the value in question (serving the poor) is one that is also addressed by individuals and agencies that are not explicitly Christian at all. What is gained in the name of Christianity if the exercise of charity becomes characterless and generic? But on the other hand, how can such a service be made more Christian without reviving all the denominational differences that frustrated the founders at the outset?

Group Discussion

For this concluding case study discussion, it might be instructive to use a slightly different format. This time, the members of your group should role-play as the Coalition Center's board of directors. Use your own city/town/region as a model and make sure that the board consists of representatives of the various Christian communities that are prominent in that locality. Each member of your group will then take the role of representative of one of those communities and will have to familiarize him- or herself with some of the principal teachings of the specific church he or she is representing. When each member of your group feels ready to share an honest and informed position representing his or her designated community, the group can convene. Your task then will be to draw up a five-year plan for the Coalition Center, resolving as best you can the particular issues raised in the case study (How should the center be staffed? What kind of governance structures should be in place? What constituency(ies) should be served? To what degree should explicitly Christian principles be moved to the foreground? Which principles? By what means should they be promoted?) as well as others that may appear to you to be relevant to this situation, based on your own experiences in your local area as well as concepts learned in this workbook and applied in other case studies.

Remember that in all your discussions, each member should represent the viewpoint of the church community whose role he or she is playing—not his or her own. The point is to foster the experience of viewing a large set of issues through the eyes of those who are different from you in some important ways, even though they may share some basic assumptions.

In your discussion, pay particular attention to the ways in which you are communicating across denominational lines. What modes of communication seem to work best in promoting fruitful dialogue? Which ones seem to impede open discussion? What can be done to improve communication? Which principles of theological reflection worked best for your group? Why? Which ones were less successful? Why? Which strategies for enhancing cultural competence seemed to work for your group? Why? Which ones were less successful? Why?

If an ecumenical Christian group already exists in your area, what lessons learned in this exercise might help you contribute to its programs or activities? If no such group exists, do you think any purpose would be served by helping to start one? If not, why not? If so, what kind of mission or charter would you recommend for such a group?

Conclusions

I hope that this workbook has been useful to you on a number of levels. First, it has been designed to serve as a brief introduction to several of the key concepts involved in the study of culture. Second, it offers an example of how those concepts might fruitfully be integrated into a more general process of pastoral reflection as it is brought to bear on the issues confronting both clergy and laypeople involved in contemporary ministry. Third, it provides a broadly comparative perspective on some of the key factors in the current debate on cultural diversity. Fourth, it offers an opportunity to reflect on those issues through case studies drawn from real-life experiences in ministry. And fifth, it suggests further readings for those interested in expanding their understanding of these matters.

I hope that the workbook does not disappoint those looking for dead-certain solutions to thorny problems. As I hope I have made clear, the study of culture should lead to an illumination of local experience in light of general trends or tendencies. As such, the only "right" answer is the one that suits the pastoral needs of the community in which you live and work. Reaching that right answer will involve a consideration of how other people in other communities have dealt with comparable problems, but the true heart of this book is the exercise of reflecting (individually—or, preferably, in groups) on the particular cultural factors at work in your own community. The discussion/analysis and questions attached to each case study are meant to suggest avenues to explore in your own discussions; they are not meant to lead you to any one universally right conclusion.

And yet it must surely be clear that I am not completely neutral as an author. My bias is unabashedly in favor of a Christianity that is open to cultural diversity and that understands that culture—in all its splendid variety—is the vehicle through which we humans must necessarily learn and communicate the truths of our faith. To segregate faith from culture is to miss the integration of action, relationship, and belief that most effectively brings the sacred and the secular domains together. In other words, I am in favor of all solutions that tend toward the fuller understanding of cultural diversity. Understanding other cultures does not require us to adopt or blend those cultures as in the old metaphor of the melting pot, but it does make it more likely than not that we will become tolerant of the wonderful fact that there remain, as there always have been, many paths to the fullest appreciation of our God and his works.

The aim of Christian evangelization is to bring Christ to the world, not to impose the culture of one part of the world on all others. And yet our imprecise understanding of the dynamics of culture has made it very difficult to carry out that commission. Indeed, it has arguably led to the creation of more problems than it has actually solved. The reflections and exercises in this workbook are offered by a pastorally oriented anthropologist as a way to better appreciate how culture, far from being an impediment to the transcendent goals of the church, actually *serves* the larger goals that Christ himself set for us, his disciples.

Notes

Notes to Introduction

1. My inspiration here is the self-proclaimed "very ordinary layman of the Church of England"—C. S. Lewis, who, in his book *Mere Christianity* (New York: Collier, 1952, vi) writes of "the belief that has been common to nearly all Christians at all times."

2. I can speak from experience with regard to Hindu groups in the United States, among whom I have conducted a considerable amount of comparative research. Hindu congregations outside of India usually do not have to deal with racial or ethnic divisions, but they are certainly faced with problems raised by diversity in the form of age (generational differences) and gender (changing expectations about the roles of women in the United States, as compared with India). Both age and gender are treated in detail as constituent parts of cultural diversity in this book.

3. Lewis, *Mere Christianity*.

4. "Identity politics" is the result of groups basing their social and political affiliations on the perception of a shared culture, language, religion, or race as opposed, say, to the ideal of a "melting pot" or otherwise pluralistic state. See Robert D. Kaplan (1994, "The Coming Anarchy: How Scarcity, Crime, Overpopulation, and Disease Are Rapidly Destroying the Social Fabric of Our Planet," *Atlantic Monthly* [February]: 44–76) for a more detailed discussion of this point.

5. DeWight Middleton (1998, 4).

Notes to Chapter 1

For more detailed information on the issues addressed in this chapter, see the items by Cenker (1996); Chupungco (1982); Foster and Brelsford (1996); Francis (1991); Schineller (1990); and Schreiter (1986); all of which are listed in the annotated references at the end of the book.

1. Gary Riebe-Estrella, 2000, "Don't Be Indifferent to Indifference," *U.S. Catholic* 65 (7): 20.

2. This point was made very clearly by David Power (1996, "Communion within Pluralism in the Local Church: Maintaining Unity in the Process of Inculturation," in *The Multicultural Church: A New Landscape in the U.S. Theologies*, edited by William Cenker [New York: Paulist Press]) in a theoretical article. This workbook represents a practical application of that position. It is also the position represented in the textbook by Kottak and Kozaitis (1999). I believe that the value of my presentation is in bringing together a theoretical, theological argument with up-to-date social science for an audience of religious professionals eager to understand the forces at work in the society in which they work.

3. Charles Foster and Theodore Brelsford (1996) report on a project, funded by the Lilly Endowment and conducted by the Candler School of Theology of Emory University, to explore diversity in various United Methodist and Presbyterian congregations. The basic message of their report is that diversity is to be embraced as a "gift," rather than dreaded as a "problem."

Notes to Chapter 2

1. Back in 1952, A. L. Kroeber and Clyde Kluckhohn, two of the leading cultural anthropologists of the day, published a volume entitled *Culture* that was essentially a compendium of all the definitions that had been used until that point. It was a book of more than three hundred pages. Although it has never been updated, it is safe to assume that a similar book published today would be at least double that size.

2. See Bohannan (1992); and Kottak and Kozaitis (1999, both listed in the annotated references) for a more detailed exposition of the principles discussed here as involved in the analysis of the culture concept.

3. See Harrison (1998); Kottak and Kozaitis (1999, 83–118, both listed in the annotated references) for a more detailed exposition of the principles discussed in this section.

4. See Barth (1969); Kottak and Kozaitis (1999, 62–82) for more detailed information on the issues discussed in this section.

5. See Kottak and Kozaitis (1999, 203–19); and Perin (1988) for a more detailed exposition of the principles discussed in this section.

6. When a group's position in a social hierarchy is believed to be inherited by ascription rather than taken on by achievement, it is technically referred to as a "caste" system.

7. The designation of a "culture of poverty" that was common several years ago has dropped out of favor with contemporary social scientists, since the attributes of poverty

are too diverse and loosely structured to constitute an integrated system that we could confidently call culture.

8. See Friedl (1975); Kottak and Kozaitis (1999, 138–71); Morgen (1989); and Weston (1993) for more detailed exposition of the issues discussed in this section.

9. There is currently considerable debate as to whether homosexuality is genetically based or socially learned. The discussion here assumes that even if there is a biological basis for sexual preference, the behaviors associated with the expression of that preference are derived from the culture—indeed, they are highly variable when comparing one culture to another.

10. See Keith (1994); Kottak and Kozaitis (1999, 172–87) for a more detailed exposition of the issues discussed in this section.

11. See Ingstad and Whyte (1995) for a more detailed exposition of the issues discussed in this section.

12. It is worth noting that the assertion of a deaf *culture* (as opposed to a "disabled" or "hearing impaired" version of mainstream culture) centers around the status of American Sign Language as a separate language. Language is the primary vehicle for the learning and transmission of culture. If ASL were nothing but a simplified means of "handicapped" conversation, its users could be relegated to a lesser status within the larger culture. But if ASL, as its advocates claim, is a language unto itself, with its own grammar and specialized vocabulary, then it becomes a way of knowing about the world, the source of the integration of learned and shared behaviors that are the primary elements in the definition of culture. Deaf people lack the ability to use mainstream language and as such are "disabled." But they can develop the capacity to use ASL and hence can become fully "abled" in the deaf culture.

13. See Kottak and Kozaitis (1999, 237–50) for a more detailed discussion of this issues in this section.

14. See Kottak and Kozaitis (1999, 251–71) for a more detailed exposition of the points covered in this section's discussion.

15. See A. Saluter (1996).

16. See Ken Bryson, 1996, *Household and Family Characteristics*, (Washington, D.C.: U.S. Department of Commerce, Bureau of Census).

17. Bryson, *Household and Family Characteristics*, 1.

18. See L. Casper, 1996, *Who's Minding Our Preschoolers?* (Washington, D.C.: U.S. Department of Commerce, Bureau of Census). It is not clear from this report, however, whether by "the South" the author is actually referring to the new, upwardly mobile Sunbelt regions as distinct from the traditional South.

19. Kottak and Kozaitis (1999, 261).

20. Reported by Kottak and Kozaitis (1999, 270).

21. See Fried (1967) for a more detailed exposition of the issues discussed in this section.

Notes to Chapter 3

See Auerbach (1994), Baumann (1999), and Fasching (1996) for a more detailed exposition of the issues discussed in this chapter.

Notes to Chapter 4

See Wuthnow (1997) for a more detailed exposition of some of the issues discussed in this chapter.

Notes to Chapter 5

See Ronald L. Johnstone (1997, *Religion in Society: A Sociology of Religion*, 5th ed. [Upper Saddle River, N.J.: Prentice Hall]) and David Cook (1994, "A Plural Society," in *Eerdmans' Handbook to the World's Religions*, edited by R. Pierce Beaver [Grand Rapids, Mich.: Eerdmans, 406–10]) for a more detailed exposition of the principles discussed in this chapter.

1. Cook, "A Plural Society," 406.
2. Johnstone, *Religion in Society*, 341.
3. See U.S. Department of Commerce, as cited in Johnstone, *Religion in Society*, 342.
4. Johnstone, *Religion in Society*, 342.
5. See George Gallup and Jim Castelli, 1989, *The People's Religion: American Faith in the '90s* (New York: Macmillan), tables 2-5, 2-6, and 2-7.
6. Johnstone, *Religion in Society*, 352.
7. See James T. Duke and Barry L. Johnson (1989, "Religious Transformation and Social Conditions: A Macrosociological Analysis," in *Religious Politics in Global and Comparative Perspective*, edited by William H. Swatos [New York: Greenwood Press]) for a more detailed analysis of the points summarized in this section.
8. Johnstone, *Religion in Society*, 363.
9. These discussion questions are adapted from Michael Molloy (1999).

Notes to Chapter 6

See Irvine (1995); Kinast (1996); Miller, Steinlage, and Printz (1994); and Young (1999) for more treatment of the issues discussed in this chapter.

1. Irvine (1995).
2. Kinast (1996).

Notes to Chapter 16

A somewhat secularized version of the older debate over the morality of divorce seems to be the current controversy about the psychological impact of divorce on children. Researchers are divided over the question of whether children suffer greater harm when parents divorce or when parents at odds with each other stay together. In either case, it is probably significant that the values of our culture lead us to put the welfare of children ahead of the concerns of the parents as individuals.

References

The following list is by no means intended as an exhaustive bibliography of materials on cultural diversity, inculturation, or the social science theory/method bearing on the study of culture. The following items are suggested simply as those sources out of many possible references that I have personally found useful and that I believe will suit the needs of the nonspecialist reader whose interest has been piqued by the discussion in this workbook. Many of these references have extensive reference lists of their own for those who are inclined to a more thorough scholarly treatment of these matters.

Auerbach, Susan, ed. 1994. *Encyclopedia of Multiculturalism*. New York: Marshall Cavendish. This is a handy general reference for issues of concern to those working in culturally diverse settings.

Barth, Fredrik. 1969. *Ethnic Groups and Boundaries*. Boston: Little, Brown. This collection of essays is still the classic statement about the nature of ethnicity and the role of ethnic identification in the modern world.

Baumann, Gerd. 1999. *The Multicultural Riddle: Rethinking National, Ethnic, and Religious Identities*. New York: Routledge. This very up-to-date publication provides an overview of the main issues in multiculturalism. The author (who is a scholar of religion as well as a social scientist) takes the position that religion, far from being a marginal issue in the modern world, is at the very heart of the search for justice and equity in a pluralistic society.

Bohannan, Paul. 1992. *We, the Alien: An Introduction to Cultural Anthropology*. Prospect Heights, Ill.: Waveland Press. This textbook is perhaps the most engagingly written introduction to the field of cultural anthropology—interesting and clearly presented for the newcomer but solidly researched enough to satisfy the expert.

Cenker, William, ed. 1996. *The Multicultural Church: A New Landscape in U.S. Theologies*. New York: Paulist Press. This volume contains a number of important theoretical and conceptual essays dealing with the challenges of cultural diversity in local congregations in the United States. The authors' orientation is mainly Roman Catholic.

Chupungco, Anscar. 1982. *Cultural Adaptation of the Liturgy*. New York: Paulist Press. This excellent introduction to the concepts and methods of inculturation includes many good case examples of the application of the inculturative perspective to liturgy, particularly in Africa and Asia.

Fasching, Darrell J. 1996. *The Coming of the Millennium: Good News for the Whole Human Race*. Valley Forge, Pa.: Trinity Press International. The author, an ethicist, argues that the Church cannot be the Church without the world of non-Christians, the world of strangers, since the heart of biblical ethics is hospitality to the stranger. His call to find "the Messiah in the stranger" is a compelling, poetic take on the values of multiculturalism.

Foster, Charles R., and Theodore Brelsford. 1996. *We Are the Church Together: Cultural Diversity in Congregational Life*. Valley Forge, Pa.: Trinity Press International. This volume is the report of an extensive research project examining diversity in church congregations (mainly United Methodist and Presbyterian) in the United States. Its emphasis is on those congregations that have successfully embraced diversity, although diversity is discussed mainly in terms of ethnicity and race.

Francis, Mark R. 1991. *Liturgy in a Multicultural Community*. Collegeville, Minn.: Liturgical Press. This very useful, concise book looks at the relationship between Christian faith and its cultural expressions, with a focus on worship. The author's historical perspective allows him to demonstrate that Christians have always dealt with cultural diversity in worship in creative and ever-changing ways.

Fried, Morton. 1967. *The Evolution of Political Society: An Essay in Political Anthropology*. New York: Random House. A classic statement on issues of power, governance, and authority.

Friedl, Ernestine. 1975. *Women and Men*. New York: Holt, Rinehart, and Winston. Although dated in some respects, this treatise is still a seminal study, one that really helped introduce the questions of sex, gender, and sexuality to the mainstream of social science in a nonpolemical way.

Harrison, Faye V., ed. 1998. "Contemporary Issues Forum: Race and Racism." *American Anthropologist* 100 (3): 607–715. This set of articles was commissioned by the American Anthropological Association from some of the leading current specialists on race and racism. Published in the foremost journal of anthropological research, it stands as the most up-to-date and comprehensive statement on these issues.

Ingstad, Benedicte, and Susan Reynolds Whyte. 1995. *Disability and Culture*. Berkeley: University of California Press. This volume was a response on the part of social scientists to the United Nations Decade for Disabled Persons. The collection of essays deals with the cultural dimension of disability in comparative perspective.

Irvine, Janice M. 1995. *Sexuality Education across Cultures: Working with Differences*. San Francisco: Jossey-Bass. This book is a very readable, useful guide to developing sensitivities in multicultural settings. Although the focus is on programs of sexuality education, the author's conceptual, methodological, and practical points are all very relevant to other contexts as well.

Keith, Jennie. 1994. *The Aging Experience: Diversity and Commonality across Cultures*. Thousand Oaks, Calif.: Sage. This monograph is a comprehensive overview of social gerontology, dealing both with substantive case studies and conceptual statements about the interplay between culture and aging.

Kinast, Robert L. 1996. *Let Ministry Teach: A Guide to Theological Reflection*. Collegeville, Minn.: Liturgical Press. This handbook is a user-friendly exposition of the theory and method of theological reflection, with numerous case studies and other illustrations drawn from a wide variety of contemporary ministerial settings.

Kottak, Conrad P., and Kathryn A. Kozaitis. 1999. *On Being Different: Diversity and Multiculturalism in the North American Mainstream*. Boston: McGraw-Hill. This concise textbook is probably the best summary and overview of the many aspects of diversity discussed in the preceding chapters; although it is the product of very careful scholarship (by one of the most prominent of contemporary American social scientists and one of his star graduate students), it is written in a very accessible style that makes it particularly useful for a general readership.

Middleton, DeWight R. 1998. *The Challenge of Human Diversity: Mirrors, Bridges, and Chasms*. Prospect Heights, Ill.: Waveland Press. This concise, well-written survey addresses the issues of human diversity by explaining how social scientists go about studying the dynamics of human interaction at both the group and personal levels.

Miller, Lynda, Theresa Steinlage, and Mike Printz. 1994. *Cultural Cobblestones: Teaching Cultural Diversity*. Metuchen, N.J.: Scarecrow Press. This workbook is a useful source for those interested in exercises aimed at promoting cultural sensitivity.

Morgen, Sandra. 1989. *Gender and Anthropology: Critical Reviews for Research and Teaching*. Washington, D.C.: American Anthropological Association. This volume reviews gender studies that have been conducted in a variety of cultures and comments on some of the general issues related to culture and gender.

Perin, Constance. 1988. *Belonging in America: Reading between the Lines*. Madison: University of Wisconsin Press. This study is an interesting take on "categories of inclusion and marginality" (also known as social class) in the United States from the perspective of a social scientist who takes psychological theory as well as cultural theory into account.

Saluter, A. 1996. *Marital Status and Living Arrangements*. Washington, D.C.: U.S. Department of Commerce, Bureau of Census.

Schineller, Peter. 1990. *A Handbook of Inculturation*. New York: Paulist Press. This treatise is a standard text on the history, theory, and method of inculturation.

Schreiter, Robert. 1986. *Constructing Local Theologies*. Maryknoll, N.Y.: Orbis Books. This analysis of inculturation is by the contemporary theologian with perhaps the best grasp of anthropological concepts and methods.

The Synod for America. 1997. "The Gospel and the Fate of Indigenous Peoples." *Origins* 27: 445–60. This article is a compilation of recent statements by various theologians regarding the issues confronting the multicultural church at the end of the millennium.

Weston, Kath. 1993. "Lesbian/Gay Studies in the House of Anthropology." *Annual Review of Anthropology* 22: 339–68. This study is probably the most widely cited overview of the anthropological approach to the cultural dimensions of the diversity of sexual orientation.

Wuthnow, Robert. 1997. "The Cultural Turn: Stories, Logics, and the Quest for Identity in American Religion." Pp. 245–66 in *Contemporary American Religion: An Ethnographic Reader*, edited by P. E. Becker and N. L. Eiesland. Walnut Creek, Calif.: AltaMira. This article, by one of the foremost scholars of contemporary religion, looks at the contributions to our understanding of the changing role of the church in modern society made by those who have studied culture.

Young, Crawford, ed. 1999. *The Accommodation of Cultural Diversity: Case Studies*. New York: St. Martin's. A valuable resource for those interested in how societies are coping with cultural diversity in places other than the United States.

Note

The United States Catholic Conference/National Conference of Catholic Bishops has published a number of books, pamphlets, and videos on "multicultural issues." The USCC/NCCB catalog lists these items under the headings "African Americans and Contemporary African American Issues," "Hispanic Americans," "Native Americans," and "Appalachia." There is also a book with accompanying video dealing with the relationship between the Church in the United States and the Church in Latin America. These resources are very good for the specific areas and issues listed (and can certainly be an important supplemental resource for non-Catholics as well), but they do seem to perpetuate the stereotype that culture is what other people have—they do not reflect a recognition that multiculturalism is at the heart of the mainstream church and must be understood beyond the context of outreach to specified minority populations.

The Web site of the National Center for Cultural Competence, which is updated regularly, provides excellent material suitable for group training, as well as current links to other Internet resources for those interested in integrating intercultural dialogue into their plans and activities.

About the Author

Michael V. Angrosino is professor of anthropology and religious studies at the University of South Florida, where he has served as chair of the Department of Anthropology and as founding director of the University Honors Program. In addition to a doctorate in anthropology, he has earned a Master of Arts degree in pastoral theology, as well as postdoctoral certification in public policy analysis. He has served as editor of *Human Organization*, the international journal of applied social and behavioral science and has been active as a consultant on cultural diversity issues and on the delivery of mental health services to a variety of Christian religious bodies.

Among other works, Professor Angrosino is the author of *Opportunity House: Ethnographic Stories of Mental Retardation; Biography, Autobiography, and Life History in Social Science Perspective; A Health Practitioner's Guide to the Social and Behavioral Sciences*; and *Anthropology Field Projects*. He is also the author of numerous articles, book chapters, and consultant reports dealing with the contributions of an anthropological research perspective on the study of the impact of formal religious bodies on the development and implementation of public policy in the United States and the Caribbean.